BEING MARRIED, DOING GENDER

Household chores, child-care and home maintenance are the practical issues around which the everyday lives of most couples revolve. *Being Married, Doing Gender* uses couples' discussions about the family chores to explore the psychological dimensions of life together. Caroline Dryden finds that most couples are keen to present their relationship as a partnership of equals, but closer scrutiny reveals that equality is an unresolved issue and the subject of much psychological conflict.

Set against the literature of gender relations, *Being Married, Doing Gender* explores marital and personal identity, gender relations and emotional experience in the lives of heterosexual couples. It will be a useful source text for scholars in psychology, sociology and gender studies at all levels.

Caroline Dryden is a senior lecturer in communication studies and psychology in the School of Cultural Studies at Sheffield Hallam University.

WOMEN AND PSYCHOLOGY

Series Editor: Jane Ussher
Department of Psychology, University College London

This series brings together current theory and research on women and psychology. Drawing on scholarship from a number of different areas of psychology, it bridges the gap between abstract research and the reality of women's lives by integrating theory and practice, research and policy.

Each book addresses a 'cutting edge' issue of research, covering such topics as post-natal depression, eating disorders, theories and methodologies.

The series provides accessible and concise accounts of key issues in the study of women and psychology, and clearly demonstrates the centrality of psychology to debates within women's studies or feminism.

The Series Editor would be pleased to discuss proposals for new books in the series.

Other titles in this series:

THIN WOMAN
Helen Malson

THE MENSTRUAL CYCLE
Anne E. Walker

POST-NATAL DEPRESSION
Paula Nicolson

RE-THINKING ABORTION
Mary Boyle

AGEING IN WOMEN
Linda R. Gannon

BEING MARRIED, DOING GENDER

A critical analysis of gender relationships in marriage

Caroline Dryden

London and New York

First published 1999
by Routledge
11 New Fetter Lane, London EC4P 4EE

Simultaneously published in the USA and Canada
by Routledge
29 West 35th Street, New York, NY 10001

Typeset in Baskerville by Routledge
Printed and bound in Great Britain by
Clays Ltd, St. Ives PLC

British Library Cataloguing in Publication Data
A catalogue record for this book is available from the British Library

Library of Congress Cataloging in Publication Data
Dryden, Caroline.
Being married, doing gender: a critical analysis of gender relationships in marriage/Caroline Dryden.
p. cm.
Includes bibliographic references and index.
1. Marriage–Psychological aspects. 2. Man–woman relationships.
3. Sex role. 4. Feminist psychology. I. Title.
HQ734.D848 1999
306.85–dc21 98-29689
CIP

ISBN 0–415–16558–X (hbk)
ISBN 0–415–16559–8 (pbk)

CONTENTS

ACKNOWLEDGEMENTS

There are a number of people to whom I am indebted for the production of this book. I would particularly like to thank all the participants in my research for giving so generously of their time. Many thanks also to Jane Ussher for her encouragement and editorial guidance, to Viv Ward at Routledge for her help and patience and to Brenda Billinghurst, Sue Mayer, Paula Nicolson and Jennifer Mason for all their practical and intellectual support along the way. The quotation from *Cold Comfort Farm* on page 107 (copyright Stella Gibbons 1932) is reproduced by permission of Curtis Brown, London. Anne McManus' poem 'wedding pest' on pp. 8–9 is reproduced by permission of the author. Finally, love and thanks to Rob Johnson for reading and commenting on each chapter, helping with the production of the final draft and generally keeping me sane!

1

A FEMINIST PSYCHOLOGICAL APPROACH TO MARRIAGE RESEARCH

CAROLINE: Do you, in terms of doing things, you know, in terms of cooking and cleaning and gardening, stuff like that, are there particular things that one of you do that the other one wouldn't or, how do you organise/

RICHARD: Yes…cook.

MARGARET: Cooking, I do all the cooking.

RICHARD: But nearly everything else [pause] it's/

MARGARET: In the house Richard'll…I mean Richard's put the hoover round this morning. Um, yes, you'll clean the bath and yes, he does everything round the house 'cept cooking. I do the ironing. I tend to do the ironing.

RICHARD: I don't iron.

MARGARET: [pause] Yeah, you say 'I don't iron!' like as if, well, I shouldn't have to iron, but it's only – you could if you put your mind to it.

RICHARD: That's – what I meant [laughing a bit like 'oh dear']. No, I don't iron and I don't cook. (a) cause I wouldn't enjoy ironing and there's no way I'm gonna do that and (b) [pause] er cooking I'm, I'm/

MARGARET: Why do you say there's no way I'm gonna do that?

RICHARD: I don't wanna be standing there with an iron. No thank you.

MARGARET: Fine! [pause] Tomorrow you do the ironing.*

The above is an extract from an interview with a married couple. What is going on in this dialogue? Are the couples, for example:

- giving me a *list of different tasks* they both do about the house?
- trying to *work out* what tasks they both do?
- *having a disagreement* in front of me about who does what?

* The following conventions have been followed in the dialogues: / indicates an interruption; a bracket linking separate lines of speech indicates overtalking; and […] on a separate line indicates that dialogue has been omitted.

- disagreeing about the supposed *reasons why* she does one set of tasks and he does another?

I think this quote is *superficially* about who does what around the house but that there is much more to it than this. I think there is a complex sub-text working between the lines of the above extract and that this sub-text can best be understood in terms of three interrelated aspects of:

- marital and personal identity
- gender power relations
- emotional experience.

This book is, in essence, an investigation of the complex sub-text of a marriage through an analysis of these three interrelated processes. The chapters are organised around a series of qualitative interviews with a small number of married couples talking together and separately about their lives and their relationships. As with the above reproduced dialogue, much of the data used focuses on the topic of division of labour in the home. The aim of the book is *not*, however, to study division of labour in marriage per se. The focus of the research is on the construction of meaning, experience and identity in marital relationships and, in particular, on the relationship between 'meaning-making', emotional experience, social power and social change. Discussions on division of labour are used extensively throughout the book because the topic had considerable relevance and symbolic significance for the couples whose experiences are investigated. As such, they provided an excellent vehicle for exploring the 'meaning-making' sub-text of couples' psychological worlds.

In writing a book about marriage for a series on Women and Psychology, it probably goes without saying that the book owes much to feminism and is feminist in orientation. This means that it also forms part of a contemporary critique of the, until recently, unswervingly anti-feminist stance of mainstream psychological research. There is now an enormous feminist literature documenting the exclusion and misrepresentation of women's experiences in social science research. Such exclusionary processes range from neglecting topics traditionally associated with women's lives, to developing general social science theories from empirical studies with male participants only, to using methods of data generation that eclipse women's lived experiences (e.g. forced choice questionnaires to test a prior, androcentric theory). Given its long and close association with the natural sciences, psychology has remained one of the hardest disciplines to 'modernise' in the face of such significant criticisms from feminists. However, the series for which this book is written bears witness to the fact that changes are finally occurring. Courses on psychology and women are now quite common in this country and extremely common in the United States. Feminist psychology in Britain is no longer a tiny fringe activity. From the milestone of Wilkinson's edited collection (1986) through to notable studies such as Griffin (1985)

Kitzinger (1987), Hollway (1989), Squire (1989), Burman (ed.) (1990), Ussher (1991, 1997), Phoenix, Woollett and Lloyd (1991), Wilkinson and Kitzinger (eds) (1995) and Nicolson (1996) – to name but a few – the launch of the international journal *Feminism and Psychology*, and the development of contemporary series such as the one this book is written for, feminist psychology is clearly making its mark.

The rest of this chapter is organised into three sections. The first section briefly outlines why I think there is a need for the type of research I will be drawing on in this book. The second section sets out my broad conceptual framework for studying marriage and the final section outlines the 'nuts and bolts' of my theoretical and methodological approach.

The need for feminist psychological research on marriage

Marriage in the public eye

The first reason why I think there is a need for research on the psychology of marriage is because the institution seems to be in turmoil viewed from a number of angles.

Statistics

Newspapers and television programmes constantly rehearse the statistical tale of doom and gloom. For a start, on current calculations, four out of every ten legal British marriages in the 1990s will end in divorce. In other words, we are close to reaching a situation where every couple getting married for the first time will have a no better than 50–50 chance of staying together until one of them dies.[1] Furthermore, although at the time of writing nine out of ten people will still marry before they are 50, marriage rates are lower than they have been for seventy years with the number declining by one-third between 1980 and 1990. Marriages where neither partner has been married before are now lower than they have been this century – less than 300,000 a year. Those who do get married are doing so later – often choosing to live together first. Remarriages now constitute around 40 per cent of all marriages. Cohabitation is increasingly becoming a substitute for (as well as a precursor to) legal marriage and increasing numbers of children are born to unmarried couples or into one-parent households.

Politics and social policy

Against the statistical backdrop of marriage in turmoil, the 1980s and 1990s have seen intense political interest in the institution and its future prospects. The British Conservative Party in their years in power positioned themselves as the party of 'traditional family values' and championed policies designed to retrench women's position in the home. In the Conservative analysis, 'the family' stood outside of the normal 'cut and thrust' of the market and 'the family' equalled one man, one woman, a legally binding contract and lifelong monogamy. Yet throughout the early 1990s, media 'exposés' continued to underline the point that Conservative politicians seemed unable to practise their own philosophy. Reports of politicians' marriage break-ups and adulterous relationships became commonplace headline stories.

Even 'traditionalists' have been unable to halt the decreasing popularity of marriage and it was, ironically, the last Conservative Government that introduced the supposedly liberalising 'Family Law Bill' which was seen by many of the Government's own supporters as likely to undermine marriage still further by making it quicker to divorce.[2] In the event, the Conservatives experienced considerable pressure from their own supporters to amend the Bill (for example, a vociferous campaign by the *Daily Mail*) and it is debatable whether the final Act is, in fact, 'liberalising'. It does, however, incorporate a new emphasis on conciliation and commentators such as Rodger (1996) have argued that, at the very least, what we have seen in the last few years is a policy move in this country away from a punitive stance on marital breakdown to an approach that emphasises mediation, conciliation and therapy. Political rows continue over the possible causes of marital breakdown and what can/should be done (if anything) to halt the tide, with some public figures, such as Mrs Justice Hale (Hale 1997), making explicit links between the current situation and women's increasing expectations of equality within the marriage relationship.

The Royals

If we needed any further public proof that there is a problem with the institution of marriage, the British Royal Family seems to have provided it with the unfolding of our own royal soap opera. Royal divorces have now become commonplace, e.g. Margaret, Anne and Andrew. And, of course, 1996 was the year of the end of a fairy tale when the marriage of Charles and Diana was officially declared to be over. The beautiful young girl became engaged to a prince. She walked down the aisle in yards of taffeta and silk. They disappeared into the sunset to produce heirs to the throne and live happily ever after. A symbol of beautiful, romantic, wedded bliss.... But then came the adultery, bulimia, reported suicide attempts, separation and public slanging matches. As the Archdeacon of York put it on *News at 10* (19 August 1996) 'The fantasy has gone of the happy family at the centre of the Nation.'

In 1997, the death of Diana served to renew public concerns about marital breakdown and the possible effects on children. Much has been made of the fact that Diana herself was from a broken home and various public commentators speculated on how this could have contributed to making her an insecure and vulnerable person. At the same time, there has been considerable attention to Diana's history of adult unhappiness and psychological ill health in her own marriage following the adultery of her husband. This has spawned a number of articles in the press and 'women's pages' on the relationship between marriage, women and psychological health.

Contradictory meanings of marriage

So what is the meaning of marriage in today's society? Confusing and often contradictory attitudes and images abound and to talk about marriage is usually to simultaneously moralise about society and about the way things *should* be. Marriage is variously depicted as, for example:

- A relationship for life (e.g. the *Daily Mail* campaign against liberalising the divorce law in this country, the Catholic Church stance on divorce).
- A relationship that may or may not be for life. For example, Giddens (1992) has argued that the Mills and Boon meaning of love as finding the perfect *partner* is currently being challenged in our society. The emphasis has now shifted to finding the perfect *relationship*, which may well necessitate moving on from time to time in serial fashion.
- A legal contract that discriminates against those in homosexual relationships (e.g. gay and lesbian rights groups have campaigned fiercely in recent years for the right to have single-sex marriages yet, in most Western countries, the law still stipulates 'one man' and 'one woman').
- A vehicle for oppressing women (e.g. feminist writers have argued that the institution is at the heart of women's exploitation in society).
- A psychological disaster area (as depicted by the proliferation of newspaper and magazine articles filled with a battery of accompanying statistics and concerns that particularly highlight psychological problems of marriage breakdown for children as well as spouses).

In recent years, then, marriage has been barely out of the public arena. Discussed, debated, rowed over, vilified, sanctified.... What is to become of this once so revered institution? What, if anything, is wrong with married people? What should be done about its declining popularity? It seems clear that a psychology related topic that merits so much public attention should be a prime candidate for psychological research.

The neglect of marriage in academic psychology

The second reason why I think there is a need for research on the psychology of marriage is because there is currently rather a strange gap. Pick up any article on marriage in the popular press or any novel that touches on the topic and you are likely to find yourself reading about phenomena such as love, pain, hate, fear, insecurity, jealousy etc. In other words, you are likely to be reading about psychological experiences. Pick up any number of mainstream psychological journals in the library and you are likely to have a long search before you find any reference to marriage at all. To read about the topic you will have to go to the clinical and applied journals (where there is a clear recognition that marital relationships can cause significant psychological problems in people's lives), the largely American interdisciplinary area of interpersonal communication, the social science disciplines of sociology and social policy or to explicitly feminist outlets. The strange fact is that, over the years, mainstream academic psychology has not been very interested in marriage.

The gap between what is of everyday psychological interest to women versus what is contained in the mainstream psychology curriculum struck me as highly alarming when I first embarked on a psychology degree in the early 1980s. I was a 29-year-old mature student. I was married and had been employed in clerical and secretarial jobs for ten years. I chose psychology because I felt that my life experience since leaving school could be a useful basis for studying the subject. I also hoped that the degree would equip me with better ways of making sense of human relations in future. During my informal interview, one of the lecturers told me that, judging by the experiences of other mature female students, there was a strong chance that my marriage would not survive the degree. He was right. It did not. Yet paradoxically, in the three years that I studied for my B.Sc., I think it is fair to say that I learned nothing more at all on the subject of marriage from the psychology curriculum.

The degree was a huge shock to me. I had not been at all prepared for the experimental design and statistics. We spent a considerable amount of time in the laboratory looking into tachistoscopes, measuring reaction times to perceptual events, wiring ourselves up to EEG machines and measuring physiological responses to noxious stimuli. Content wise, the curriculum seemed to be dominated by cognitive and physiological psychology and a lot of theories about the behavioural patterns of monkeys, rats and pigeons. We rarely covered anything that seemed to be of any direct psychological relevance in terms of my own experiences. The most we covered on the family was in developmental psychology and a third-year option on interpersonal communication. In the former, it quickly became obvious that as the focus of research was primarily child development, family interaction (usually mother–child) tended to feature in the journals only to the extent that it shed light on, for example, learning processes or personality development in the child. In the latter, marriage clearly had a place on the research agenda but the theories we encountered seemed strangely removed from anything I could relate to in my own life (either in my own or friends' marriages). Studies were invariably 'quasi-experimental', for example tick box questionnaires or structured laboratory observation, and they invariably seemed to produce superficial or one-dimensional findings. Yet I knew from reflecting on my own and my friends' experiences that marital relationships are likely to involve highly complex, often contradictory and extremely personal feelings – seemingly impossible to trap within the strictures of a questionnaire or the rigid boundaries of an experimental observation.

I studied for my degree in the early 1980s and I am now better able to articulate why the discipline couldn't at that time address a topic that seemed so important to me. First, marriage is not really a topic that you can do experiments on. Writers such as Giorgi (1970) were actually arguing two decades ago – but no-one much was listening then – that psychology as a discipline has been hopelessly 'method driven', meaning that a topic has tended to be considered of interest *only* if it is amenable to experiments (or a quasi-experimental approach). A watered down 'quasi-experimental' approach such as tick box questionnaire is also unlikely to do more than scratch the surface of complex and potentially contradictory feelings and emotions. Second, marriage is primarily about a *relationship* and this would not endear the topic to a discipline that has for so long taken as its major project the internal workings (or behaviour patterns of) the *individual*. Even in social psychology, where the greater part of this century has been spent trying to understand group processes, most of the time the focus for research has been the *individual* within the group (e.g. Tajfel and Turner's attempt to explain intergroup conflict in terms of individual cognitive processes. See Hogg and Abrams 1988 for a review). Third – almost too obvious to mention – marriage is a topic that has always been seen as a 'woman's issue', much more closely associated with women's than men's lives. (And this despite the fact that, in this society at least, it is still legally defined as a union between one woman and one man.) This connection is guaranteed to have kept it low on the popularity stakes in a discipline whose history has been to a large extent the history of the exclusion of women's experiences (Squire 1989, Henwood and Pidgeon 1995). Last, but not least, I have already made the point that marriage is about emotional experience and the strange fact is that psychology has never really been about emotional experience (Frosh 1989). For the greater part of this century the academic psychology focus has been predominantly on *behaviour*. Traditionally, behaviourism – essentially the experimental study of rodents (e.g. see Watson 1924) – involved the quest to uncover the laws presumed to underpin human behaviour chiefly through the study of other species such as the rat. Rats, presumably, were cheaper and easier to experiment on than humans but, of course, they were unable to talk to researchers about their thoughts and feelings. Behaviour, in any case, was the only factor of interest because it was the only feature of the animal's psychological processes that was directly observable and therefore amenable to description and measurement. In the behaviourist's paradigm, emotional experience was, at best, relegated to the concept of a conditioned physiological response (e.g. Seligman's (1974) work on depression and the notion of learned helplessness) and at worst ignored entirely.

With the demise of behaviourism came the birth of *cognitivism*. Cognitivism developed from renewed interest in proposed 'innate' differences between species – e.g. bees appeared to have a much better innate sense of direction than rats – and led to the inevitable conclusion that living creatures are not all capable of learning the same things and do not all *think* in the same way. So the study of behaviour *as an end in itself* eventually gave way to the study of mental processes – e.g. memory, attention, mental maps, schemata, attitudes and stereotypes. But in this cognitive refocusing of the problem there has still been little room for the study of emotional experience. What we have seen is a transformation of the researcher's 'human being' from a bundle of conditioned responses to a computer-like rational information processor. In fact, I would agree with Frosh that (with the exception of psychoanalysis which has always stood outside of mainstream psychology) the history of Western psychology this century can be seen as the history of the exclusion of emotions from the research agenda.

In short, then, marriage is about complex human relationships, women *and men*, gender issues and emotions. The very aspects that seem to have made it unappealing to the discipline made it seem endlessly interesting to me when I was a mature, married student wrestling with the complexities of everyday life. I have not changed my opinion. In fact, I now believe very strongly that the topic should be of *central concern* for the discipline. After all, as I said earlier, over 90 per cent of the population will marry at least once in their lives and the number of people whose lives have been touched by marital breakdown, separation and divorce continues to rise. You only have to glance at the popular press to discover very quickly that psychological aspects of marriage are of considerable interest to the general public.

My conceptual framework for studying marriage

wedding pest

far be it
from me
to impose
my crystal clarity
on those who
resent it
who prefer
obscurity
obfuscation
and illusion

we know love
is about smoothing
and soothing
and not using
your brain

but mine
is trained
in truth

so better
stick to it
and not confuse
the issue
by tissues of lies
about
paradise

instead
of chains
that marriage
represents

(Anne McManus)

There are two strands to my conceptual approach to studying marriage and I will look at each in turn.

Gender power relations and marriage

The first thing I want to do in setting up my own framework for studying the psychological dimensions of marriage is to locate the relationship within an analysis of gender power relations. I have talked so far about marriage in terms of the personal aspects – the emotional dimensions of an intensely private relationship between a woman and a man. However, this intensely private relationship between a woman and a man is also cemented by a legal contract stipulating what is and what is not possible in order for a union to be called a 'marriage'. As I have already pointed out, in this society one of the key features of this union in the eyes of the law is that it has to involve one woman and one man. Polyandry or polygyny, for example, are not currently acceptable in British law. Neither is an official union between two women or two men although this position is currently being fiercely challenged by gay rights groups. From this perspective, at the very least, marriage is a socially organised institution that is fundamentally about gender, and gender relations in this society are not currently equal.

Writers were making connections between marriage and gender power relations long before the rise of the Women's Liberation Movement in the 1960s in the Western world. For example, Cicely Hamilton's (1909) book, *Marriage as a Trade*, served as a powerful indictment of the institution in relation to women's suffrage. In the early part of this century, other famous figures were taking 'pot shots at marriage' – e.g. Isadora Duncan, whose comment that 'any intelligent woman who reads the marriage contract, and then goes into it, deserves all the consequences' is now immortalised on a postcard.

Feminist historians and novelists have written about how, until the turn of the century, women in this country were treated by the law as the property of their husband. They did not have the right to vote in this country until 1918 and then only women over 30 were enfranchised. Women between 21 and 30 were considered 'too flighty' and did not receive the vote until 1928 (Anderson and Zinsser 1988, p. 366). Discriminated against in the employment sector, a woman needed to marry to survive and yet the marriage contract itself discriminated against her and rendered her forcibly financially dependent on her husband. The vestiges of the notion of 'ownership' can be seen today in the tradition of a woman taking a man's name when she marries. Although it is no longer compulsory, it is still possible for a woman to include the word 'obey' in her marriage vows to her husband.

With the onset of the Second World War, women were called on in great numbers to take over the jobs left by men when they went to fight. For many women, such opportunities for employment provided new opportunities for financial independence. Yet with the end of the war, these same women were pressured to move back out of the labour force to make way for returning soldiers. New emphasis was placed on women's role in the home as housewife and mother and, whilst for working-class women such a total break from the labour market was often not a realistic option, the notion of woman as homemaker and carer became the 'ideal' to be aspired to.

In the last thirty years, feminist (usually sociologically oriented) interest in marriage and gender power relations has intensified and, taken together, does not make cheerful reading. In particular: (1) the housewife role has been continually linked with depression for women (e.g. see Friedan 1965; Gavron 1966; Bernard 1982; Oakley 1974; Ussher 1991). (2) Study after study reports that British and American wives and heterosexual cohabitees as a group *still* have major responsibility for household tasks, childcare and caring for other family members even though a high proportion of these women are also in paid work outside the home (e.g. see Van Every 1995; Bruess and Pearson 1996; Press and Townsley 1998). (3) Housework, childcare and other caring responsibilities have been characterised by feminists such as Delphy and Leonard (1992) as *unpaid labour* and there is now a sizeable sociological literature on ways in which housewives have been exploited by society for various aspects of their labour (e.g. see Duncombe and Marsden 1993, 1995 on 'emotional labour'). (4) Wives are still economically disadvantaged in marriage (Pahl 1989) and, reciprocally, still discriminated against in the world of paid employment (Beechey 1987; Witz 1993). (5) Statistically, women are much more at risk of being attacked, raped or murdered in their own home by their husband or male partner than they are of being attacked, raped or murdered by a stranger. (It was only in 1991 that a law was passed in this country making rape in marriage illegal.) Husbands are much less at risk than wives of being attacked or murdered by their spouse (Ussher 1997; Bruess and Pearson 1996).

Having just painted the very bleak picture above, I want to return to the personal aspects of marriage and reiterate the point that the relationship is, for many women, not *just* about gender power relations. It is also supposed to be about factors such as intimacy, sharing, love, etc. In order to address this point, I want to outline the second aspect of my approach.

Interpersonal and intergroup relations

> The relationship of man to woman is like no other relationship of oppressor to oppressed. It is far more delicate, far more complex. After all, very often the two love one another.
>
> (Rowbotham 1973, p. 34)

The second aspect of my theoretical framework for the study of marriage involves a recognition of the above point and a plan for dealing with it. Jenny Williams (1984) once characterised marriage as situated at the 'crossroads' between 'intergroup' and 'interpersonal' relations (intergroup as denoting the dynamics of (unequal) gender relations and interpersonal as between two unique individuals). I think this characterisation provides a useful way into a psychological investigation of the topic. It allows us to recognise the importance of simultaneously exploring both these dimensions within a marital relationship and this is what I intend to do in this book.

Such an approach rarely seems to have been taken in the clinical and interpersonal communication literatures. In fact, throughout both these literatures, there seems to have been a distinct reluctance to enter Jenny Williams' crossroads. With one or two notable exceptions (e.g. see the clinical work of Schneider 1990, Urry 1990 and the communications work of DeFransisco 1991 and Berk 1985) three common patterns tend to occur in both areas: (1) Heterosexual couples are frequently 'conceptually uncoupled' from the social world they inhabit with no mention of the possibility that male–female interaction might not take place on a 'level playing field'. Writing in this tradition is typically 'gender blind' with explanations of husband–wife interaction/problems couched in terms of unisex/personalised individual properties and the need to acquire better communication skills. (2) Gender issues are recognised but 'rendered safe' by being translated into either natural or culturally acquired *differences* that are treated as part of husbands' and wives' makeup. Writing in this tradition typically talks about 'gender differences' as puzzling cultural or biological 'peculiarities' that we need to work round (e.g. *Men are from Mars, Women are from Venus,* Gray 1997). (3) The possibility that gender power relations/gender inequality may be relevant is acknowledged in the form of a metaphorical note through the marital letter box. This might take the form of a token chapter in a text book on relationships talking about 'the feminist perspective' or a brief discussion about 'role changes' in heterosexual relationships – usually kept quite separate from discussions of intimacy or romantic love.

I think there are two principal reasons for this failure to enter Williams' crossroads in marriage research. First, it is a conceptually difficult thing to do. This book is an attempt to grapple with some of the conceptual problems inherent in such a project and, in so doing, I try to follow the lead of Bhavnani and Phoenix (1994). These writers have argued in relation to their work on racism that a major project for psychologists *should be* continually to question what it means to be an 'individual' and, in so doing, continually to challenge the boundaries between concepts of 'individual' and 'social'. (In this connection, my work also has much in common with the interesting social constructionist work of Burns and Griffin (1996) and Kitzinger and Powell (1995) on infidelity.)

Second, I think there is more to the problem than conceptual difficulty. I think there is also an emotional problem. Clark (1991) has suggested that the lack of attention to experiential aspects of the marriage relationship in feminist sociology may be because such research could imply some tacit approval of an institution that feminists would not want to be seen to support. The problem is that the whole area of heterosexual relationships is bound to be emotionally charged, particularly for researchers who identify as feminists and who are married, planning to marry, or are in heterosexual relationships. I think it is also interesting here to reflect on discussions I have held over the years with university students on the topic of marital relationships. One thing that has struck me forcibly throughout these discussions has been the reluctance with which students will make connections between the subjects of gender inequality and the relational aspects of marriage. This reluctance has manifested itself in group discussions on women's studies courses and other units where students have already had plenty of prior contact with feminist literatures, are well read in feminist literatures and keen to make connections elsewhere (e.g. gender inequality in the workplace, women's experiences of oppression in the psychiatric system). Whilst there might be a general agreement amongst students that 'the family generally' might have been a problematic institution for women over the years – often a place of violence or a mechanism of economic oppression – and that there might have been problems for women over the traditional roles of housewife and mother, when asked to brainstorm what marriage means to them, most student groups will come up with concepts such as 'security', 'commitment', 'sharing', 'give and take', 'companionship' and – less commonly – love. In a seminar conducted on a women's studies unit during 1997, we had an interesting discussion on my perceptions of this issue. Some of the younger students in the group (all women) said that, whilst they could acknowledge that gender inequality was likely to be related in a number of ways to marital relationships, they didn't want to believe it, they wanted to believe it was a phenomenon of the past – e.g. their parents' marriages – and they certainly didn't want to believe that it could be relevant to them. Some of them said that they were looking forward to the prospect of marriage sometime in the future and they didn't want to spoil this anticipation. This also ties in with the recently published findings from Walkerdine et al.'s (1997) longitudinal study on adolescent girls, who tended to express positive views on marriage and see it as part of their future aspirations. Some of the older married women clearly valued the intimacy and companionship they derived from their relationships and were unhappy about appearing disloyal in making connections with feminist arguments. Again, this ties in with Ros Coward's (1992) observation that women in their thirties who have a critical analysis of gender relations usually, nevertheless, treat their own marriages as 'okay'.

In short, there is no doubt that heterosexual relationships are extremely important to a great number of women in this country, as are notions of love, closeness and intimacy. As a heterosexual woman myself I identify with these concerns. There is also no doubt that gender is currently an important organising principle for inequality in this society. It is equally the case that it is conceptually and practically problematic to bring these two contradictory dimensions together, not least because Jenny Williams' crossroads is dangerous territory. The recognition of this contradictory position formed the starting point for constructing the main elements of my study. I outline these elements below in the final section of this chapter.

The theoretical and methodological elements of my research

A qualitative method

The first thing I needed to do when designing a study of marriage was to find a method that would be sensitive enough to cope with difficult, complex and potentially contradictory issues. I decided to focus on a small number of married people and use an in-depth qualitative interviewing approach. I wanted to *really listen* to what people had to say about their married lives since the potential for listening is a major advantage of qualitative over quantitative methods (Duelli-Klein 1983). I interviewed seventeen couples in all (see Chapter 2 for details). Interviews were only very loosely structured (around topics such as family, friends, children, daily life etc.) because I wanted people to bring up areas that they themselves considered relevant throughout discussions. I interviewed all the couples twice with an eighteen-month gap between the interviews. All the first interviews were conducted jointly with the couple. If spouses were happy to do so, second interviews were conducted with each partner separately. In two cases couples chose not to do this and second interviews with these couples were therefore also joint.

Interviews were long (all at least an hour – often lasting over two hours). From these interviews I generated a vast amount of conversation data from married people talking about their everyday lives. In aiming to *really listen* to people's views, beliefs, stories etc. of their marriages, however, I did not treat the conversation as a simple or straightforward medium for conveying information about people's lives. To attempt to use qualitative data in this way would, I believe, involve missing a number of important social and psychological points about human interaction and sense-making processes. In order to begin to explain better what I mean here, and to begin to outline what I *did* do and why, I want to pick up in advance a theme from my interview analysis – equality versus inequality.

When I asked married couples in my study a direct question about gender relations or gender inequality, the overwhelming response was quite similar to the reaction of students in class discussion referred to above. People were happy enough to talk about the existence of inequality in the workplace but much more cautious about making connections with the marital relationship (and it is also worth noting here that I was cautious about asking them for fear of offending by implying that it might relate to their marriage). If there was a link made between marriage and gender inequality, this was usually placed somewhere else, perhaps another sector of society, as in the following extract from the interview with a couple I will call the Evanses:

GORDON: I think in middle-class um, families, and I s'pose we, because of our jobs and so on, and our attitudes, would be considered middle class, I don't know. But certainly people like us, expect a much more balanced partnership between husband and wife. I think in working class families, from what I know, um, there's still fairly sort of – prejudiced, chauvinist attitudes by men. Er, you know – 'I wouldn't do that. That's women's work' you know. That means they'd never change a nappy on their own children. They never cook any food. So on and so forth. I think it's er – middle-class and educated people realise that that's hardly the way to to make a balanced relationship.

Or the link between marriage and gender inequality was sometimes located in the past, as in the joint interview with the Scotts:

TOM: My mother used to do the cooking and the washing up and all the housework as well as her other job while my father tended to do, you know, typical male tasks if you see what I mean. You know there was a clearly defined role. You know, like with us now, we tend to share a lot more things don't we.

And again, in the separate interview with Liz Walters:

CAROLINE: Do you think marriage has changed?
LIZ: Definitely [long pause] a more equal – partnership – than when the wife used to stay at home all day.
CAROLINE: Is that true of your marriage?
LIZ: Yes, I think so. We both do equal amounts.

Conversation as active and constructive

The point I want to draw out from the above dialogue is that I do not think people were simply 'passively reporting to me the equal nature of their relationship' in these extracts. I think there was a lot more to it than this. Rather (in discursive psychological terms, e.g. see Potter and Wetherell 1987) they were *actively doing something* in their conversation. Specifically here, they were *actively making a distance* between their own relationship and relationships outside of their own world. These other relationships were then made a kind of repository for problems of inequality. So, for example, with Gordon Evans above, the 'problem' is located in a class-ridden, stereotypical image of a working-class man and, by implication, their own (middle-class) relationship is equal. In *really listening* to what I think people were saying to me about their marriages, I want to underline here that the emphasis throughout this book is on the active and constructive nature of talk.

Constructing reality and identity

In treating conversation as active and constructive, the third element of my own approach involved following Mead's (1934) symbolic interactionist work and exploring possible links between meaning-making and the interactive construction of identity. In particular, I borrowed from the work of Berger and Kellner (1964) on the notion of the marriage as a key identity-forming relationship. In order to explain more about what I mean, I want to continue the theme of equality versus inequality.

In locating gender inequalities 'somewhere else' – e.g. in another sector of society or in the past – the couples I interviewed usually simultaneously emphasised the sharing properties of their own relationship *by comparison* and, again, this comparative process has been identified by Wetherell and Potter (1991) and Billig (1991) as a discursive practice adopted by speakers for the purpose of distancing themselves from accusations of racism. Furthermore, an emphasis on the sharing properties of the relationship invariably translated into an account of shared household labour (as is reflected in the three earlier extracts). In emphasising the shared nature of household labour there was also a strong tendency for couples to describe their domestic arrangements to me in fairly 'gender undifferentiated' terms, as in the following interview with the Prices:

RICHARD: Well I can only speak for our, for for us. I mean I [pause] although my Dad does the housework as well. But I'm sure [pause] his era was – the women do the housework, the men go out to work. Well I s'pose a lot of blokes still – feel that way. In fact a lot of my friends obviously do. <u>But um [pause] personally I – the house is as much my responsibility as Margaret's and in fact it's usually me that does – you know –we split it 50–50.</u>

In this extract Richard, in comparing his relationship favourably with those of the past and, also, with those of some of his friends, seems keen to emphasise that who does what in the house is a quite 'gender undifferentiated' issue. This theme of 'gender blending' of household tasks can also be seen reflected in the earlier extracts from Gordon, Tom and Liz above and there were numerous other examples of this in interviews, as in the following dialogue from Nick and Sally Freeman:

NICK: So we [pause]...sometimes I cook a meal. Sometimes you do something.

SALLY: [both talking together] – sort of housewife – house – er housework chores, that sort of thing, I mean there's no real demarcation. We generally do [pause] whatever.

NICK: Mm.

Women seemed particularly keen to emphasise the gender undifferentiated nature of division of labour as with the extract from Sally above, although, when a more traditionally gendered pattern was presented, even here, the emphasis was very much on the overall sharing properties of the arrangement as with Sarah and Malcolm Anderson, where I had just asked them who did the housework:

SARAH: Well – I do really but that's basically because Malcolm's out at work most of the time and with overtime that's why I mean you can't expect him to do it anyway but he does help – on holidays if we – if we're both here.

MALCOLM: Not enough probably but er/

SARAH: Or if we are – sort of on holiday say on a caravan holiday then we – we muck in together don't we?

MALCOLM: Yeah, yeah, yeah.

SARAH: you know. But then I'm not very good at decorating or anything like that so that all comes on Malcolm, but I mean that's – the arrangement isn't it really.

MALCOLM: Yeah.

Even in the above extract where there is an appeal to a traditionally gendered division of labour, Sarah is keen to make the point that when they are on holiday there is much more 'mucking in together'. Arguably, the implication here being that the sharp division of labour that exists at other times is not inherently for any reason to do with gender but rather to do with practicalities.

The main point I want to draw out here is that, in telling me about the gender undifferentiated or fair nature of division of labour, I think couples were also essentially 'meaning-making' about their identity as a couple as they talked to me. To borrow an expression from West and Zimmerman (1991) I think they were 'doing' identity work. West and Zimmerman in their work on gender difference, view gender as 'not a set of traits, nor a variable, nor a role, but the product of social doings of some sort' (p. 16). These authors have focused on the notion of identity work to refer to gender identity but here I co-opt it in this book to talk in the first instance about *relational* identity. In the above extracts, wives and husbands were constructing relational identities that were characterised by modern principles of democracy, sharing and equality. Throughout this book I try to treat human identity not as some kind of fixed property that the individual metaphorically carries around in their pocket. Rather, I view identity as a kind of multi-faceted, fluid and interactive process. So, for example, I will be looking throughout the book at three interrelated aspects of identity work for the married people I interviewed – personal, relational and gender.

Focusing on the contradictions

The fourth aspect of my approach involves an explicit focus on contradiction and inconsistency. So, for example, in every interview I conducted, statements concerning gender undifferentiated patterns of division of labour were contradicted by other aspects of couples' discussions (both separately and together) of the detailed nitty-gritty of everyday life. Even though in my sample two women worked full time outside the home and ten worked part time – with all but one couple having at least one child under 5 – the overall picture to emerge from all the interviews was that women still had major responsibility for housework and child-care – even where husbands were unemployed (and I will be giving a number of examples of this in later chapters). And of course, this finding is in line with other qualitative sociological studies discussed earlier, whether the couple have young children (Backett 1982; Lewis and O'Brien 1987), are retired and the children have left home (Mason 1987) or if the couple have only recently married and are both working full time with no children (Mansfield and Collard 1988). In fact, as journalist, Louisa Young, put it (*The Guardian*, 9 September 1997) commenting on findings of the ongoing British Household Panel Study:

> Women do more when they are working and the man unemployed, when they are working longer hours than the man, when they are both employed full-time – whatever the set-up.

This more traditional view of division of household labour emerging in the interviews can be glimpsed through an extension of the extract already reproduced on page 16 from the interview with Sally and Nick:

NICK: So we [pause]...sometimes I cook a meal. Sometimes you do something.

SALLY: [both talking together] Sort of housewife – house – er housework chores, that sort of thing, I mean there's no real demarcation. We generally do [pause] whatever.

NICK: Mm.

SALLY: There's certain jobs that I tend to do, more frequently than you – like I mean/

NICK: Cause you're here.

SALLY: That's right. But I mean things like the car, you see, and DIY. I mean, I can change a plug and all that sort of thing, but [pause]. I would say that, I mean – well also Tony [their son] is very very good at that sort of thing. I mean he does, you know, he does all the wiring and that sort of thing.

CAROLINE: Does he?

SALLY: Oh yes. But I mean, I would say, that that, it just happens to be that you tend to do – don't you, that sort of thing really, more than me, don't you, whereas I – tend to get stuck with the washing or – I don't know. I just sort of [pause]. Just how it is really. I think sort of being here every day.

Here we see Nick and Sally moving from a 'gender undifferentiated' arrangement to one that sounds suspiciously gendered – albeit Sally explains this in 'practical' rather than 'gendered' terms. Again, a similar pattern emerges in an extension of the conversation (p. 14) with Tom and Emma:

TOM: My mother used to do the cooking and the washing up and all the housework as well as her other job while my father tended to do, you know, typical male tasks if you see what I mean. You know there was a clearly defined role. You know, like with us now, we tend to share a lot more things don't we.

EMMA: Oh yes, I mean/

TOM: Because basically we're both working you know. I know my, both my parents were working as well. But still there were certain – things that each of them did. You know.

CAROLINE: Yeah. How do you think you've come to that decision to share, the two of you?

EMMA: Well, I don't think it was a sort of conscious decision was it really? We sort of just

TOM: [We just sort of drifted into it like.

EMMA: [evolved into doing things.

TOM: Yeah.

EMMA: I mean [pause] [slight laugh] one thing that Tom always does, or nearly always, is the washing up. I don't like – I can't stand washing up – he does [that.

TOM: [Which suits me cause I don't like cooking.

As with Sally and Nick's dialogue earlier, the account Tom and Emma begin to portray here starts to feel quite traditionally gendered with Tom taking responsibility for a fairly well-defined male province of washing up. (Although here again, the explanation for a fairly traditional split between chores is again not couched in 'gendered' terms, but this time in terms of 'personal taste'.) Then, five minutes after the above exchange, I ask the couple if they ever have any disagreements over housework:

TOM: [Yeah, frequently.

EMMA: [Oh I should think so! [all laughing]

TOM: Yeah well you know, sometimes, you know, Emma comes home, does the cooking and I come down, eat the meal and then, the washing up [she laughs]. Now, it's my job to do the washing up but sometimes [pause] I don't do it. I get a bit of er, you know, 'earache', for that really.

Finally, in my separate interview with Emma a year later when Tom had left his job, Emma told me at one point that when they had both been working full time Tom had not pulled his weight in terms of household tasks. (Although, again, interestingly, she told me this in the sense that this problem was now in the past – i.e. she distanced her relationship from any current involvement with this problem.) She also told me, however, that 'she' was now considering paying someone to come in and do the housework – i.e. responsibility for household tasks clearly lay with Emma. And, of course, numerous sociological studies have attested to the fact that it is still predominantly women who have the worry of the general management of the household affairs in heterosexual relationships (see Van Every (1995) for a summary).

In short then, attention to the detail of spouses' conversation implied a pretty traditionally gendered pattern of household labour with all the couples I interviewed that seemed to belie statements of gender blending made elsewhere in conversation. What is more, interviews were full of examples of conflict over division of labour and there was *no* example in my study of a couple that did not tell me stories during the course of their interviews about disagreements on the subject. Some rowed in front of me.

In focusing on contradictions, I did not treat them as a nuisance or problem for my analysis. Rather, I viewed them as a way in to exploring the richness of everyday life. I wanted to examine ways in which accounts of everyday life might be linked to identity processes but *also* – a point not made until now – how everyday interaction of this kind might be linked to wider social processes and to the notion of gender power relations. If, in meaning-making, we can construct various versions of reality, it also needs to be said that some versions of reality may contradict others, and that some are likely to have more chance of being 'made' than others. Crudely speaking, this is because when we talk we do not sit at the drawing board making it all up from scratch. We weave together our conversation using social material *already in the public domain* – albeit, in using this material we perhaps have the potential to transform it.

In short, I used a focus on contradictions as a way in to the meaning-making of married life and, in so doing, I viewed contradictions as a kind of 'gateway' to the crossroads of a marriage discussed earlier. For me, the meaning-making entered into by wives and husbands when discussing aspects such as division of labour in the relationship at one level *formed* the crossroads between the contradictory dimensions in a marriage of gender power relations on the one hand and intimacy, love and sharing on the other. In forming the crossroads, versions of reality had the potential to push apart or bring together opposing or contradictory dimensions of a relationship and to simultaneously transform their meaning.

A focus on 'realistic relativism'

In attempting to focus throughout this book on ways in which married people constructed versions of identity and, relatedly, reality, I take the philosophical position that it is impossible to describe reality in a way that is stripped of human meaning. This does not mean, however, that I think there *is* no reality in which human meaning is anchored or that it is pointless to *try* to give meaning to that reality. This implies that, although I do not to treat conversation as a simple vehicle for getting at a 'truth stripped of human meaning', neither am I trying to study conversation as 'all there is' – disconnected from situated thought, action and a material world.

Reality and power

As writers such as Weedon (1987) have pointed out, versions of reality will be likely to contain within them the power to seriously affect an individual's ongoing life chances, circumstances and *experiences.* For example, a version of reality that constructs the traditional homemaker/breadwinner division of labour as 'fair' is likely to make it hard for a woman to avoid cleaning the house – at least without feeling guilty. Throughout this book I try to demonstrate ways in which I think particular versions of reality that married people were constructing might be having ongoing material and emotional consequences for these people's lived experiences.

Reconstructing the psyche

In talking about the material and emotional aspects of people's lives, I want to return to a point made earlier in this chapter that an important aim in this book is to focus on the emotional experience of married people. I said earlier that behaviourism and, subsequently cognitivism, had taken turns in keeping emotions off the academic psychological agenda over the last few decades. We have recently witnessed a concerted attack on cognitivism from within critical social psychology and the broader field of social constructionism where, in its extreme form, a third refocusing has taken place, this time to the notion of human being as textual product (e.g. see Edwards and Potter 1992; Potter and Wetherell 1987). I have drawn heavily on insights from much of this writing in outlining my approach to marriage so far and texts such as the above have formed a powerful and extremely important critique of the problems with traditional psychology. However, it has to be said that the move to social constructionism and discourse analysis in psychology has done little more than the previous paradigms to put emotional experience on the academic agenda. More than this, a lot of social constructionist writing treats the human being as, to all intents and purposes, an empty vessel psychologically speaking (Burr 1995). To focus on emotional experience is, by such an analysis, to miss the point and to be no better than traditional psychology. In what follows, then, I want to in a sense *try* to miss the point. I *want* to reconstruct the psyche in my work because, as a psychologist, I can see no point in doing this kind of research in any other way. In this, I follow the work of Nicolson (1996). Nicolson's belief is that:

> to exclude a *sense of the individual* from critical and feminist psychology is unproductive in the long term, and increases the widening gap between feminist psychologists and the women who might benefit from their analysis of gender-power relations.
>
> (p. 5)

Also, I think that focusing on the complex interrelationship between meaning-making, action and human emotional experience can yield considerable explanatory power for making sense of processes of gender power relations in marriage. I will try to demonstrate this point throughout the book.

A reflexive approach

This brings me to the eighth aspect of my approach to my research. I tried to be 'reflexive' in my study. This means I needed to bring to bear in my study an analysis of my own role in the process of sense making about relationships. For example, returning to the subject of 'distancing' discussed above, it is worth noting here that I 'helped' people to locate gender inequality outside of their own marriages – by phrasing questions in broad or general terms. I helped people to do this because I *believed* that failing to make this 'distance' could represent, in Goffman's terms, a 'threat to face' for people (e.g. see Goffman 1982). I *believed* this, as a woman, from my own experience of being married and interacting with friends who are married. In the same way, in *really listening* to what people said, I was not a computer or an android but a human being. Listening is an *active*, not a passive process and by its human nature must involve assumptions and interpretations on the part of the listener. I have said above that my philosophical position here is that reality can never be *known* in a way that will somehow be uncluttered by human '*meaning-making*'. It is impossible to shrug off my humanness as a researcher to study human processes. I offer the finished product of this book, then, not as 'truth' or 'fact' but as a form of 'meaning-making' that I hope some people will find illuminating, interesting, and, if possible, useful.

The characteristics of 'the moment'

The final aspect of my approach to my study involves focusing on the interview context itself. In saying that I view talk as active and constructive rather than a simple tool for reporting reality, this means that I needed to try to understand as much as possible about what people might be attempting to do or achieve when they talked to me, what kinds of possibilities the interviews offered people and what, if any, problems they presented. This means I needed to ground my microanalysis in a broader analysis of the *demands of the moment*.

In focusing on the particulars of the interviews as a social context and in trying to get to grips with what status they might have presented to the married people who participated in my study, I want to argue that it is useful to think in terms of three broad social forces: (1) obligations, (2) possibilities and (3) problems. These three forces can best be seen as shaping the framework from within which interview conversations took place.

Obligations

The notion of social obligation links most closely to existing literature on marital relationships. When I went round to talk to people as a stranger wanting to find out about their relationships, I generated a situation in which couples' relationships were essentially on display to a member of the outside world. There is now a good deal of evidence from sociological studies that people 'put on a public face' when they discuss relationships, i.e. they present their relationships in a 'socially acceptable' way and I think people who participated in my study experienced this pressure. To borrow another term from West and Zimmerman (1991) I think interviews placed couples in a situation where they became publicly *accountable* to make sense of their relationships to me as *equal*. Again, in this approach, I am not treating relational accountability as a kind of 'problem' that needs to be controlled for or screened out and neither am I suggesting that it was some sort of freak phenomenon restricted to the peculiarities of my research interview. Rather, I am suggesting that I made this aspect of everyday sense-making in interaction particularly salient through conducting the interviews. First, I had come to talk to people about their *marriage* rather than other aspects of their lives and, therefore, I had sensitised people to the topic and probably made them 'self-conscious' about it. This self-consciousness was sometimes expressed in humorous asides. For example, Amanda Wright said when her husband brought the tea into the room during their interview, 'you can pour tonight as it's equal opportunities!' In the same way, in my joint interview with Sarah and Malcolm Anderson, Malcolm asked if I would like coffee and Sarah said:

SARAH: Oh, you're going to put it on are you? [laughing]
MALCOLM: Oh yeah. Show off tonight [laughing a bit]. Create a good impression for you [all laughing].
SARAH: Ahh [as in 'poor thing']. No, he does quite often make a cup of tea [laughing]. It's not just cause you're here.

Second, as is obvious from the above comment from Sarah, my being a female researcher from the university who most of the participants in my study clearly perceived as being a 'career woman' was likely to have heightened a concern with equal opportunities issues and a pressure to make sense of the relationship to me in these terms.

Possibilities

Although interviews created a situation where couples were likely to feel some social obligation and accountability for the status of their relationships, half of the couples whom I interviewed voluntarily contacted me to take part in the study and this suggests they had some prior interest in participating and finding out more about what I was doing or in being helpful to me in my studies. In the event, most of the people I interviewed (not just those who had voluntarily contacted me) told me they found the interviews interesting and were usually keen to carry on past the appointed time. I think interviews provided a number of interaction 'possibilities' for spouses. For example, there was the possibility of finding the act of participating in the research study intrinsically interesting. There were other possibilities, however. For example, the interview provided a forum for discussing topics that the rush of everyday life might ordinarily prevent. There was also the possibility for a spouse to listen to what their partner had to say about topics they might not usually discuss. Related to this, there was the possibility of putting across an argument to a spouse, to challenge a spouse's views, or to perhaps enlist my support in any of these actions.

Problems

However, if interviews provided possibilities they also provided problems and I would argue that this is true of any human interaction. For example, in this context, reflecting back to the notion of social obligation mentioned earlier, some of the possibilities presented by the interview, e.g. to discuss, debate, challenge, etc. might have the potential to create relational accountability problems through creating an image of the marriage not 'fit for public consumption'. Relatedly, problems could present themselves in terms of 'threats to face' but also could be more to do with issues of power and control.

In fact, the potential problems presented by interviews were, I think, legion, and need to be seen as an outcome of often highly contradictory obligations versus possibilities arising from the demands of the moment. Because the rest of the book is essentially taken up with focusing on problems, I do not want to say much more here. I will, however, make the point that, although interviews presented possibilities and problems for both wives and husbands, I think interviews were more possibility related for wives and more problem related for husbands. To return briefly to the extract I used at the beginning of the book, when Richard told me in that extract that he did not iron I think he was simultaneously digging for himself 'a bit of a hole'.

In Chapters 3 and 4 I want to use the framework of obligations, possibilities and problems as a starting point for exploring in some detail first women's, and second men's accounts of division of labour. In doing this, I should reiterate that I am not focusing on division of labour *as an end in itself* but rather because, first, the topic was clearly important to the couples I interviewed and, second and relatedly, discussions on this topic were usually about much, much more than who did what around the house. Before I proceed with this, however, I want to sketch out in Chapter 2 a brief biography of the couples who participated in my study.

2

A FEMINIST BIOGRAPHY OF MARRIED COUPLES

In this chapter I want to convey a sense of social biographical background which later chapters will not be able to do justice to because of pressure of space and continuity of argument. In doing this, I attempt to reiterate the point made earlier that in any one given moment of life human action is 'always already social' (Henriques et al. 1984). I try to capture this 'sociality' by working outwards from an analysis of the demands of the moment discussed in Chapter 1 to an attempt to piece together a brief biographical account of couples[1] gleaned from what they told me in the interviews. The couples were selected through a form of opportunity sampling.[2] In the event, all participants were white but came from a range of class backgrounds. Most couples had at least one child under 5 years old and the average age of participants was in the mid thirties. Wives were, in all but two cases, younger than their husbands. The biographies have been placed in the main text of the book rather than in an appendix because I think they provide a way of helping the reader to hold on to the 'whole people' in this study, whereas later chapters tend to cut across whole people to draw out themes. The biographies can, however, be read as a chapter in their own right or can be treated as a reference to dip into 'as and when' useful. The biographies are written from my interpretation of the wives' perspectives and the underlying assumptions behind my interpretation are feminist. They are organised in alphabetical order for ease of reference.

Sarah and Malcolm Anderson had been married for thirteen years at the time of my first interview. Both in their mid thirties, they had three children aged 12, 8 and 2. The 2-year-old, they told me, had been a 'bit of a surprise'. The couple lived in a large house on the edge of an inner-city area. Malcolm was educated at a local comprehensive school, and then trained in a skilled manual occupation in which he had been working ever since. Sarah was educated at a local school where they focused on secretarial training. On leaving school she worked as a secretary but gave up shortly after getting married in preparation for their first child. Apart from the local play-group, Sarah had not been in paid employment since that time. The local play-group paid £2.50 for a morning's work. Sarah clearly lacked confidence in her abilities and was particularly concerned about whether she would have the skills to undertake any other paid employment. The couple were one of the few explicitly to label their relationship as traditional in terms of division of labour. However, Sarah was clearly highly ambivalent about her role as housewife and caregiver and there was evidence of conflict around division of labour in the marriage. Sarah also told me she experienced depression related to pre-menstrual syndrome. I approached the couple and asked if they would take part in the study.

Janet and Simon Campbell had been married for eight years at the first interview and they were in their early thirties (with Simon slightly older than Janet). They had two children, aged 6 and 2, and they lived in a comfortable house on the edge of an inner-city area. Both educated at grammar school, Janet had subsequently studied for a further education qualification. She then spent six months working abroad, after which time she did 'odds and sods', she told me, including various secretarial jobs. Simon went into a skilled occupation on leaving school and worked his way up through various companies until, a while after meeting and sharing a flat with Janet, they moved to their present locality with his job. Shortly after this, he set up his own company. Janet finally left work to have their first child and had been at home ever since. By the time of the second interview, when the youngest child had started nursery school, Janet was beginning to look for part-time office work to fit in with her child-care duties. Although the couple had a joint bank account, Janet talked about family money as 'his money'. She also had major responsibility for housework and child-care. She told me she lacked confidence and was a 'worrier'. He told me he liked to 'poke fun at society' by dressing his daughters in blue. I approached the couple and asked if they would take part in the study.

Karen and Will Craven had been married for five years at the time of the first interview and had two children, aged 3 years and 10 months. Karen was in her late twenties and Will in his early thirties. Karen had been educated at private school whilst Will had attended a comprehensive and had entered farming aged 16. Karen's family were farmers and owned two farms between them. Karen and Will lived in and ran one of these farms. In my first interview with the couple Karen tells me that, for her father, having three daughters was 'not a disappointment I don't s'pose but…'. She also talked about Will as being the next best thing in her father's eyes to a son. Karen experienced post-natal depression after the birth of their first child and told me she still feels quite depressed from time to time. She also told me she lacked confidence. Although Karen told me she got involved in farm business, she had complete responsibility for housework and child-care and clearly had little direct power in overall decisions concerning the farm. The couple were openly affectionate to each other in front of me. The couple contacted me voluntarily.

Joan and Peter Docherty had been married for seven years at the time of the first interview. Both in their early thirties (Joan slightly older than Peter) they had two children, aged 5 and 2. They had recently moved to the area with Peter's job and lived in a modern house in a pleasant rural area. Joan had worked in a professional capacity before leaving paid employment to have their first child. She had major responsibility for housework and child-care and an ongoing problem between the couple, I was told, was that Peter was not interested in children – or family life. This clearly caused a lot of conflict between the couple and gave Joan a lot of distress. Joan seemed unhappy during both sets of interviews with the couple. The couple contacted me voluntarily.

Rachael and Gordon Evans were in their late thirties (with Gordon slightly older than Rachael) at the time of the first interview. They had been married for nine years and had two children, aged 7 and 2. The couple lived in a comfortable house in a city area. After leaving school, both spouses had undergone professional training and until Rachael left work to look after the first child they were both working in the same occupation on comparable salaries. The couple told me that Rachael had been admitted to psychiatric hospital on the birth of their first child:

CAROLINE: Right. So what happened at that time then? Did you look after Ian?

GORDON: There's a mother and baby unit at [the hospital].

CAROLINE: Oh, I see.

GORDON: And they keep them together, and they make them do all the sort of changing and the feeding and whatever – and eventually, you know, she got better.

Rachael had been suffering off and on from depression ever since and talked a lot about how she missed her career. She was now working part-time and looking for full-time employment. Rachael had the additional burden of caring for a disabled mother and clearly had overall responsibility for housework and child-care. I approached the couple and asked if they would take part in the study.

Sally and Nick Freeman had been married for thirteen years at the time of the first interview. Sally was in her late thirties and Nick in his early forties. They had four children, aged 11, 8, 6 and 2 and the last child, they told me, was 'a bit of a shock'. The couple lived in a comfortable semi-detached house in a pleasant residential area. Both spouses were educated at grammar school and subsequently undertook further professional training. Before Sally left work to look after their first child, the pair were in comparable professional occupations. In the intervening years of child-care, Sally had been working part-time in a related occupation to the one for which she had specifically trained. She clearly had overall responsibility for housework and child-care. She talked a lot throughout the interviews about wanting to get back into full-time work and there was evidence of considerable conflict around division of labour. I approached the couple and asked if they would take part in the study.

Joanna and Bernard Hardy had been married for just over two years at the time of the first interview. In their early thirties (both the same age) they lived in comfortable housing in a rural area. Bernard had been to university and both spouses were in professional occupations at phase one of my interviews. Joanna was pregnant and by the time of the second interview the baby had arrived safely and was just over a year old. The Hardys were both fairly open in discussing ways in which gender inequalities might impinge on their marriage and in this way they were unique in my study. They were keen to tell me in the first interview that when the baby arrived they would avoid traditional roles. However, eighteen months later when I visited them again it was clear that this had not really happened. Joanna had been the one who had given up work to look after the baby and the reason given for this was financial. She had subsequently started a business from home which involved her working long hours. However, she was only able to do this because they could afford to employ a nanny and a cleaner. They did tell me that as soon as Joanna got the business running efficiently, the aim would be for Bernard to leave his job and join her. However, Bernard admitted that over the last year it had been Joanna that had taken ultimate responsibility for their child. Furthermore, he acknowledged that this had been a terrible strain on her. The couple were openly affectionate to each other in the interviews. The couple contacted me voluntarily.

Gillian and Patrick Henderson married when they were both still at university, nine years previously, and at the time of the first interview they were both in their early thirties (with Patrick slightly older than Gillian). The history of their subsequent employment mirrors other couples already mentioned. Gillian left university with a good degree but finally ended up working as a nanny and a helper in various play-groups. Patrick, on the other hand, became a highly paid worker in a professional occupation. The couple had three children, aged 3, 2 and 3 weeks old at the time of the first interview. They lived in a spacious and comfortable house in a pleasant semi-rural area. Gillian clearly had major responsibility for housework and child-care. Patrick was keen at various points in the interview to present himself as a 'modern man' by saying, for example, that he had been keen for Gillian to keep her own maiden name and bank account when they married. Gillian was, however, clearly financially dependent on Patrick and talked about concerns she had stemming from watching female friends whose husbands have left them with the children, all the responsibilities and no money. Gillian told me in her second interview that she had been suffering from post-natal depression. She clearly lacked confidence and seemed very depressed and vulnerable. The couple contacted me voluntarily.

Marion and Tim Hughes had married thirteen years ago when she was just 18. Now in their early thirties the couple had three children aged 10, 8 and 1. Although situated in an affluent middle-class suburb, Marion and Tim lived on a council estate and Tim had been unemployed off and on for about six years. At the time of the first interview he was in fact working on a six-week casual job. He told me there was a possibility this work would be extended. However, when I returned to visit the couple for the second time, I was told that he had left this work soon after my previous visit and had been unemployed ever since. Marion had given up her factory work to have their first child and, apart from a spell of part-time manual work, she had not been employed since.

Marion clearly did all the housework and childcare and Tim seemed quite keen to highlight this point.

The couple had a history of severe financial difficulties and, between my first and second visits, the bailiffs had, I was told, tried to evict the family because of a 'hiccup' with the social security payments. Tim was rude and abusive to his wife, particularly in the second interviews. I became uneasy when interviewing Tim on his own and terminated the interview early. I felt very sorry for Marion. The couple contacted me voluntarily.

Carol and Tony Matthews had been married for ten years at the time of the first interview. Carol was now in her late twenties and Tony in his early thirties. They had three children under 6 and had lived in an inner-city area for most of their married life. Originally training in a skilled occupation, Tony had been made redundant three years before the interview. Money, they told me, was 'tight'. By the time of the second interview Tony had obtained semi-skilled employment. Carol had given up her first and only job (in an office) to look after their first child. She worked part-time at the local play-group. At various points in both interviews she told me how much she missed her job and how much she would love to return. Carol clearly had sole responsibility for housework and child-care and this was the case at both interviews (i.e. whether Tony was unemployed or employed). Both spouses talked about the family money (including family credit payments the couple received) as 'his money' and this seemed to be a cause of anxiety for Carol. I approached the couple and asked if they would take part in the study.

Heather and Gerry Morris had been married for eight years at the time of the first interview. In their early thirties, Heather was slightly older than Gerry. They had two children, aged 6 and 2. They lived in a semi-rural area in a small, modern house. Gerry worked in a clerical occupation and until Heather gave up work to look after their first child she had been earning more than Gerry. Since leaving full-time employment Heather has worked part-time as a childminder.

Following the birth of their first child, Gerry became very depressed and withdrew from having anything to do with child-care. He would not attend the birth of their second child because he was worried this might precipitate a further bout of depression and told me he lacked confidence. Heather clearly had major responsibility for housework and child-care. She told me she lacked confidence and said she thought this was partly because 'motherhood is looked on as being – not quite the thing'. She told me that it would terrify her to go back to her old job. The couple contacted me voluntarily.

Margaret and Richard Price had been married for seven years at the time of my first interview and were in their early thirties (with Richard older than Margaret). They had two children, aged 5 and 18 months and they lived in a comfortable semi-detached house in a rural area. Margaret had undertaken specialist training after leaving school and Richard had entered a public-sector occupation in which he had been able to build a good career. Margaret had given up her job in order to have their first child and had subsequently returned to work part-time. The extent to which Richard participates in housework and child-care was hard to determine but it is clear that the major responsibility rests with Margaret and that there was conflict between them here. The couple also had a long-running disagreement about the extent that Richard went out on his own – with Richard saying he felt he was 'not allowed out enough'. At the time of the interviews the couple were seeing their GP about 'the problem of Richard's temper' and Margaret seemed very distressed about the state of their relationship in both interviews. The couple contacted me voluntarily.

Emma and Tom Scott were the only couple in my study with no children. Married for four years at the time of the first interview, Emma and Tom were in their late twenties (Tom older than Emma) and both had been to university. At the time of my first interview both couples were working full-time in professional occupations. They lived in a comfortable cottage in a rural area. Emma's career was clearly important to her, although it was only recently that she had been able to embark on the work she wanted to do because for the duration of their marriage they had been moving around the country with Tom's job. By the time of the second interview with the couple, Tom had resigned from his job and was looking for another post. Although the couple were keen to emphasise the sharing qualities of their relationship, Tom's involvement in housework seemed to stop at the washing up and there was evidence of conflict around division of labour. At the final interview with the couple, Emma told me she was thinking of employing a cleaner. Emma talked at one point about her ambivalence about being a woman and, particularly in relation to mothering and child-care, said that women are 'born with a big disadvantage stuck on your life really'. The couple were openly affectionate to each other in the interviews. They contacted me voluntarily.

Wendy and Neil Spencer had been married for just over fourteen years at the time of their interviews and had lived since then on an estate in an inner-city area. Both were in their late thirties (with Neil older than Wendy). The couple had three children aged 11, 9 and 18 months. Both had attended local comprehensive schools. Following this, Neil had taken an apprenticeship and had been employed in a skilled trade ever since. Wendy told me that she had spent two weeks at college once on a work experience course. However, when she left school she was unable to go to college and went instead into badly paid office work. She left work to have their first child eleven years ago and had been at home ever since. Recently, she had undertaken training and was about to register as a childminder. She clearly had sole responsibility for housework and child-care and Neil seemed keen to accentuate his lack of involvement in these aspects.

The interview with Wendy and Neil was extremely difficult. I approached Wendy through the play-group. At this stage she told me that although she was happy to be interviewed she was not sure what Neil would say. She suggested that I make an appointment with her and go round anyway (the couple did not have a telephone). When I arrived, Neil had agreed to participate but he was practically monosyllabic at times and Wendy and I took turns to coax him into saying things. Neil left the house shortly before the end of the interview and Wendy and I then continued to talk without him – something she seemed quite keen to do. At the end of the interview she underlines her economic vulnerability when she says 'I would *never* go back to be with parents again after being married. I mean, if I could afford not to um – I wouldn't go back home.' Wendy clearly lacked confidence and worried about a number of aspects of her life, including her relationship. I did not ask for an interview at a later date with the couple because I felt it might be upsetting for Wendy.

Cathy and Brian Thompson had been married for nine years at the time of my first interview. In their late twenties (with Brian slightly older than Cathy) Cathy was just 18 when they married. They had two children, aged 5 and 3, and they lived in a small terraced house in an inner-city area. Brian had been educated at grammar school and had subsequently gone on to study for clerical examinations. Since then he had been employed in the public sector. Cathy had been educated at a comprehensive school and had worked in an office until she left work to have their first child. At the time of my first interview with the couple, Cathy was working part-time in catering work. Subsequently she obtained part-time clerical work. Cathy was the only woman in my study who consistently openly challenged her husband for his lack of involvement in housework and child-care. They had arguments on this topic in the interviews. I approached the couple and asked if they would take part in the study.

Liz and Mike Walters had been married for five years at the time of the first interview and they were in their late twenties (Liz) and early thirties (Mike). The couple had two children, aged 2 and 9 months, and they lived in a semi-detached house in a pleasant city area. Both spouses had been educated at local comprehensive schools and Mike was now working in a technical occupation. Liz had trained in a health-related occupation after leaving school and had left work to have their first child. In the intervening period between the first and second interview with the couple Liz had returned to work on a part-time shift-work basis. Liz clearly has major responsibility for housework and child-care. The couple presented particularly contradictory images of their relationship to me during the interviews. At one point Mike describes himself as a 'chauvinist'. I approached the couple and asked if they would take part in the study.

Amanda and Jim Wright had been married for four years at the time of my first interview. Amanda was in her late thirties and Jim in his early forties. They had one child at this time, aged 21 months. By the time of the second interview a second child had been born and was 6 months old. Amanda and Jim lived in a small terraced house in an inner-city area. Jim had been to university but told me that he had a history of alcoholism, although he said he now had this under control. He had been working in a semi-skilled occupation for the last 16 years. Amanda had been to a comprehensive school and had then worked in a shop. Amanda had a history of illness and had recently developed a mobility disability. Until meeting Jim she had lived at home with her parents and they married when she was 35. She told me that she had felt fortunate in meeting Jim and said she expected her friends had thought she was 'probably one of these left-on-the-shelves'. Amanda was the full time caregiver in the family and told me that her disability would prevent her from re-entering the employment market. She clearly had overall responsibility for housework and child-care although the couple told me that there were certain things Jim had to do because of Amanda's disability. Amanda told me that she had been depressed off and on since the couple had been married, initially because she felt lonely and isolated and then later because she felt she couldn't cope with her role as caregiver. Amanda talked about the family money as 'his' money and they both talked about Jim 'giving her housekeeping'. I approached the couple and asked if they would take part in the study.

Drawing the above biographies together, I want to underline the following general points:

- In the sixteen cases in my study where the couple had children it had been the woman who had given up full-time work to look after them.
- The majority of women had earned less than their husbands before having their first child. All the women with children were at the time of the interviews financially dependent on their husbands.
- Twelve of the women in my study were engaged in paid employment, ten part-time and two full-time, during the period when I interviewed them. Of the remaining five women, most were engaged in voluntary activities of some kind in addition to their child-care responsibilities.
- Whether women were working full-time, part-time or were full-time caregivers and whether men were working full-time or were unemployed it was in every case the woman who had major responsibility for the home and (except for the couple without any) for the children.
- As I stated in Chapter 1, there was *no* example in my study of couples who did not admit to some level of conflict around division of labour.
- Seven of the women (and one man – Gerry Morris) told me explicitly that they had been, or were currently, suffering bouts of depression. Other women described experiences that sounded very much like depression.
- Nearly all the women, at some stage in the interviews, talked about feelings of lack of confidence or loss of identity brought on by motherhood and child-care. Only one of the men (Gerry Morris) talked in these terms.

In summary, my aim in this chapter has been to give the reader an overview of the couples who participated in my study. They are, of course, hardly representative of some kind of 'generalised population' of married couples with young children. In particular, all the couples were white and all came from a fairly narrow geographical area. It is therefore vital to underline that I am not attempting to make crude and inappropriate generalisations in this book to some homogenised 'general population'. Rather, I follow Van Every (1995) in quoting Dorothy Smith's point that 'any story…bears traces of the social relations in which it is embedded' (Smith 1990, p. 217, referenced in Van Every 1995, p. 4). In attempting to trace the 'characteristics of the moment' in Chapter 1 and the specifics of the couples in my study in this chapter, I have aimed to provide a basis for beginning to tease out aspects of the social relations embedded in these stories. I will discuss in the final chapter what I think are the broader implications of the stories I develop throughout this book.

3

WIVES AND THE STRUGGLE TO CONSTRUCT RELATIONAL EQUALITY

> The contradictions between female expectation of equality and the reality of inequality, and between male slogans of mutual responsibility and the retention of the old role assignments, are sharpening.…Thus we are situated at the very *beginning* of a liberation from the opportunities and contradictions. Consciousness has rushed ahead of conditions.
>
> (Beck 1992, p. 104)

Using the biographies of the previous chapter as a springboard, in this chapter I commence my 'micro-analysis' of marital identity, gender power relations and human emotional experience in marriage by focusing on what the women I interviewed were doing when they talked about conflict in their marriage – or when they engaged in arguments or challenges with their husbands.

The women I interviewed obviously viewed our discussions as presenting a good opportunity to talk about important aspects of their relationship – in a way that they may not often have had the chance to do. Although quite a few of the husbands showed interest and involvement in the interview discussions, it was predominantly the wives who seemed most engaged with the topic. That wives should show more interest in a study of marriage than husbands is not surprising given that, as I pointed out in Chapter 1, marriage is a topic that has been linked much more closely with women than with men. Women's pages in newspapers, women's magazines and novels aimed at women are full of stories of heterosexual romance, marriage and – more latterly – cohabitation. Women are traditionally 'expected' to talk openly about feelings and relationships and to take an interest in this 'emotional dimension' of life. It is also interesting to note here that two of the women I approached through the play-group were concerned that they would not be able to persuade their husbands to participate in the study. One of these subsequently phoned me and said her husband was not prepared to talk to me. The other woman's husband did agree to the interview but he was monosyllabic through a great proportion of it and left before the end. In a third and fourth case (both couples who voluntarily contacted me through letters I sent out) one husband was verbally aggressive to his wife at various stages and I curtailed the separate interview with him because I felt uneasy. One wife 'forgot' to tell her husband I was coming the second time because she said there had not seemed to be a 'good moment' to mention it.

A major possibility that interviews provided for women, I think, was to discuss conflict – either with spouse and me in the joint interviews or with me in the separate interviews. Conflict frequently appeared to be related to housework, home maintenance, child-care, or caring more generally. I began to think that these discussions of conflict over division of labour were a vehicle for discussing much more than the purely practical aspects of married life and I have therefore used these discussions as the basis for this chapter. It appears that the topic of division of labour often enabled women to try to work out *for themselves* the psychological status of their relationship and, in the process, to challenge the existing status quo. However, in challenging the status quo, there was also evidence that women felt a simultaneous pressure to present the relationship as *already equal*.

I think women's challenges to the status quo of their relationships can best be seen as created and shaped out of the tripartite psychological forces of obligations, possibilities and problems outlined at the end of Chapter 1 and in this chapter I use the framework of obligations, possibilities and problems as a way in to exploring women's challenges in some depth. The aim is to develop a simultaneous understanding of both the psychological and social meaning of women's discussions about conflict. In doing this I aim to begin to shed some light on the dangerous territory at the crossroads of a marriage. The chapter is organised into four main sections: Cautious challenges, Balancing the books, Internal debates at the crossroads and Open challenges.

Cautious challenges

The first thing to say about women's discussions of conflict around division of labour is that, although they were extremely frequent, they were also, as the title of this section suggests, frequently conducted in a very cautious way. In the following extracts from the interview conversations, I want to start to unpack the nature of this caution by identifying two simple conversational devices that tended to be used by women when discussing such conflict. In doing this, I want to emphasise that I am teasing apart strands of complex and interconnected processes for illustrative purposes. As my analysis progresses, I aim to 'put the bits back together' to give a better sense of the complexity.

Distancing

The first simple conversational device often used by the women when discussing conflict over division of labour involved a simple distancing process already introduced in Chapter 1. The best way to explain what I mean here is to give some examples. The first extract is taken from an interview with

Rachael Evans. I had just asked her whether she thought that roles in marriage were changing:

RACHAEL: Um [pause] I mean most of the students that I get on Thursday nights – the men are incredibly sort of traditional. And that you know/

CAROLINE: What – this is the adult literacy class?

RACHAEL: Yeah – and the bloke cooks – that's really sort of pushing it you know. Really, I mean even among them I mean they [pause] would say oh well yeah, you know, I might cook. It seems that cooking, for men, you know, is now quite acceptable isn't it. You get a lot of blokes cooking on television and that sort of thing. I've never come across men that dust.

CAROLINE: No [laughing]. 'Men that dust'! No – yeah.

RACHAEL: You know. I've never met a man that dusts.

CAROLINE: No – yeah.

RACHAEL: Um – er – so what am I saying – that [pause] superficially there seem to be – there are some changes aren't there. But [pause] I mean I, I – I imagine if you interviewed every wife in [city], you know, across the sort of social strata and whatever, you wouldn't find many men that cleaned the loo would you. So I – I think superficially they appear to have changed.

In the above extract, Rachael seems to be having 'a bit of a go' at men but she is nevertheless talking in general or depersonalised terms. It is also worth emphasising here that I posed the question in this way – i.e. I asked about marriage 'generally'. However, it is also interesting to note that, although Rachael appears to be talking generally, it is significant that she mentions cooking, dusting and cleaning the 'loo'. In their joint interview, Gordon, Rachael's husband, talked at length about how he is very keen on cooking exotic dishes (see DeVault 1991 for an interesting account of the gendered nature of food production) and how he wouldn't dust. However, by depersonalising this story, she creates a boundary between her own marriage and 'marriages out there'.

The following extract is taken from a joint interview with the Andersons. I had just asked Sarah Anderson whether she thought she would go back to work. Sarah Anderson, as I pointed out in Chapter 1, presented her relationship in 'traditional' terms quite early on in my first interview with the couple. She stated that this division of labour was fair because Malcolm was at work and she was at home – i.e. it was a practical rather than a gender issue. It is interesting to note here, however, that Sarah had childminding and play-group duties that she did not mention in this original justification of fairness. It is also interesting to note that I also overlooked Sarah's childminding and play-group work when I asked her the question below and I will return to this point later. This extract is taken from my second (joint) interview with the couple:

CAROLINE: Do you think you'll go back to work when you um…

SARAH: I'd like to [go back to work] yeah. Yeah. Not just for financial reasons but [pause] I s'pose that I'd like to do something. I've been, left work now nearly fourteen years, it's a long time.
CAROLINE: Yeah, yeah. What – you'd go into secretarial work would you?
SARAH: That's what I done before I had the children but obviously I'd have to sort of, brush up. But I mean I'm not too bothered at anything really, you know, just for a few hours. I couldn't cope with full time work and a house and a family. I – I haven't got that sort of energy.
CAROLINE: No [laughing]. Right.
[Malcolm doesn't say anything.]

And then, later in the interview when we are talking about role reversal, I ask her what kind of problems she could envisage with this:

SARAH: Well I – I wouldn't mind working, providing everything was done in the house. That's what worries me cause I think if I g– do go back to work, I mean [pause] I don't wanna have to come home and start cooking and cleaning and – you kn– you know. I think a role reversal's okay, providing everybody does exactly [pause] what needs to be done. You know, but I mean [he and I saying: mm] say a wife goes out to work and the husband's home, he's been sat down all day [pause] smoking, watching tele [me laughing] nothing's been done! I get – you know, I think oh well, that's not really on. But [um…
MALCOLM: [Mm.
CAROLINE: Yeah, yeah.

In this extract, then, Sarah is careful not to address her comment directly at Malcolm and she does this by illustrating her point in increasingly hypothetical terms. 'Say a wife goes out to work and the husband's home…' It seems likely, however, that her comments are aimed at 'having a bit of a go' at Malcolm. It is noticeable that he keeps very quiet throughout this exchange. It is also interesting to note that Sarah's hypothetical man smokes and watches 'tele' all day. Earlier in the interview I was told that Sarah often tries to get Malcolm to stop smoking and that, furthermore, Malcolm watches a lot of television, which can be a point of conflict between them. By not directly naming Malcolm as the man in the story, however, Sarah distances him from the account and therefore avoids the problem of calling him to account for his behaviour and – by implication – failing in her obligations to present her relationship as equal.

In sum, distancing was a common way for women in my study group to discuss division-of-labour issues and I have used the above extracts to try and demonstrate this process. Depersonalised or hypothetical accounts of conflict or discussions of potential future arrangements did not directly threaten the 'here and now' of a woman's own relationship. However, there were a lot of occasions within my interviews where women were clearly keen to discuss the specifics of conflict with their spouses and therefore had to bring issues into the 'here and now'. Directly relating them to their own life situations was clearly difficult for women but still seemed to be something that women often wanted to do. However, there was invariably considerable caution in *so explicitly* discussing friction which brings me to the next practice women tended to engage in as part of challenging cautiously.

Minimising

If women challenged division-of-labour arrangements in their own relationship and, by implication, made a criticism of their husband's behaviour, they frequently prefaced or peppered their comments with minimising phrases such as 'it's little things', or 'daft, silly things' etc. The following extract from a separate interview with Karen Craven demonstrates this process:

KAREN: Um [pause] I think sometimes perhaps he's um [pause] he's a bit critical, of me. Or perhaps I take, I think, I take things very personally, you know. He's – sometimes he mightn't mean it the way I think he means it you know but – I sometimes feel that he's always – criticising [with slight laugh] you know or [pause] commenting sort of thing you know.

CAROLINE: Can you give me a for instance?

KAREN: Um [pause] um [pause] well silly daft things you know like [pause] even um, his meals and things like that, he'll say you know, well why do you do that? and sort of thing. An I thought, you know, I was thinking I was doing it, you know, to make it better and he, he says oh you know you [pause] you know, I, um, what'd I do this morning? Oh I – I made the to– I made the toast for his poached eggs, cause he was going to the [Agricultural Show] thing and I thought well, he has to be gone at half past nine so I thought well I know I [pause] I'll do the toast for his poached eggs and I put it in, I buttered it and I thought oh you know, all nice melted butter and everything and I put, put a top over it you see and I thought well that'll stop it drying up in the oven, an of course he took – he said what did you put the top over it he said you make me toast soggy and I though well you know, I did that to – to make it better an there he is criticising me you know [I'm laughing]. It's only a stupid, daft thing but [he comes in the room] go away! [laughing].

WILL: [He asks if we want coffee and then hovers around.]

KAREN: Its only a stupid thing you know but I think I p'rhaps take things too personally I don't know. I take things to heart [he mumbles 'yeah']. Shut up! [laughing]

Karen uses a version of 'silly daft things' three times in the above extract and, arguably, the overall effect is to tone down the importance of the conflict in order that it becomes socially acceptable to talk about without creating a bad impression to me.

However, it is clear from an overview of all three interviews with the Cravens that this issue is not necessarily quite as unimportant as Karen makes out. Karen and Will told me in different ways, separately and together, about this 'problem' and Karen's account above suggests they might have rowed about it that morning.

Here, then, I think that Karen – by using the minimising 'silly daft things' – is trying to preserve an overall account of fairness whilst simultaneously trying to rehearse the basic facets of the conflict to herself (and me) and at some level try to work out whether her grievance is legitimate (and perhaps even enlist my support).

In sum, this practice of toning down direct challenges by minimising comments was, as with distancing, extremely common in my interviews. The two types of conversational practices were sometimes used in tandem. Taken together, they created the possibility of cautious challenge to the status quo of a relationship. I think these practices enabled women to take up the possibility of discussion and debate around delicate issues whilst being mindful of social obligations to the construction of relational equality (and further examples of these processes will be seen in later extracts). However, the processes identified above are fairly 'light-weight', and sometimes not effective enough on their own to keep challenges cautious. In such cases, or if challenges went too far, women often engaged in a range of other practices to as it were 'balance the books' and I will turn to these next.

Balancing the books

If challenges to the status quo of a relationship became too overt or explicit, there were four main practices that women tended to engage in to balance the books of fairness. I will go through them in turn, giving one or two examples from the data for each.

Traditional claims of fairness

The first way in which challenges would be diffused or counterbalanced by women in conversation was by simply drawing on a traditional claim to fairness. For example, above I have used an extract from an interview with Rachael Evans where she talked in depersonalised terms about the unlikely situation that men would clean the loo. A bit later in my discussion with Rachael, I ask her directly about her own relationship and the following discussion ensued:

CAROLINE: What about in your own marriage?
RACHAEL: Mm.

CAROLINE: Do you think that gender roles are an issue for you in any way, or not?

RACHAEL: [pause] Um [pause] well, getting back to the tangible things, yes I mean there are certain things I mean it would be – I mean Gordon would never clean the loo. I mean he would say that he would, I mean I s'pose he'd pour some bleach down it occasionally you know but, with the sort of bad aim our sons have got, you know, he wouldn't, he wouldn't even think of it. And – I know I'm at home and he's at work so in fact that sort of scotches your question but I mean I don't think he would even think of it, even if I were working full-time. Um [pause] I don't know though, I mean on the other h– on the other hand I mean he might put the hoover attachment on and go round all the sort of plaster work or something which is a thing that

CAROLINE: You wouldn't do it?

RACHAEL: I would never do so [pause]. I s'pose he's fairly sort of enlightened, he just hates housework. [both laugh]

In this account, when I ask Rachael about her own situation she says that Gordon would be highly unlikely to clean the loo. However, no sooner has she implied some sort of lack of egalitarianism in her own marriage than she engages in book-balancing activity by drawing on a traditional claim to fairness (albeit stating the fairness of the situation in practical 'I'm at home and he's at work' terms). Her remark that 'that sort of scotches your question' also suggests her heightened sense of obligation in this context to as it were deflect a potential implied criticism from me. Yet even within this construction of fairness Rachael still seems to be debating the status of the situation. She then appears to have a brief debate with herself around whether or not the situation would be satisfactory if she worked full time. She seems to leave the answer to her debate unresolved, concluding by balancing the books again, this time in personal choice terms – 'he's fairly sort of enlightened, he just hates housework'.

Drawing on a traditional claim of fairness was a common book-balancing practice in my interviews. It is also interesting to note here that Rachael's brief debate about whether or not Gordon would do more if she was working full time does not involve a discussion of her present employment (and this is true in Sarah's discussion of role reversal earlier). In the above extract from Rachael's interview, despite her part-time work, she draws on this traditional discourse to justify Gordon never 'cleaning the loo'. She then briefly muses about what might happen if she worked full time, and appears unable to decide. Rachael herself had just been for an – unsuccessful – interview for a full-time job and was clearly concerned about this issue. Sarah Anderson's hypothetical discussion of the husband sitting around watching television and smoking whilst his wife is at work also demonstrates a level of concern on her part about this issue. In fact, the issue of what would happen if a woman returned to full-time work seemed an issue for a lot of the women and raised concerns about the future. This brings me to the next theme – that of stretching traditional claims of fairness.

Stretching traditional claims of fairness

Janet Campbell had this to say about what she called the 'nightmare' of having overall responsibility for the children in her household:

> JANET: Um [pause] I mean certainly, if I was working – if I had taken on this – if this job had materialised [she had applied for a job that didn't come about], um, I think probably I'd be saying a few different things [at the moment she says she might moan but nothing more] because I think the pressure would be – would be much greater really. Um [long pause] which is one, you know, I mean, one reason why I'm quite pleased I'm, I'm not actually doing it, because I don't particularly like, operating under pressure.

The practical aspects of this concern are obvious. How many people would thrive on the idea of working all day and then coming home and doing the housework, the cooking and looking after the children? However, whilst a woman is not in paid employment, the traditional 'breadwinner–homemaker' ideology will just about stretch to make sense of the situation. When the woman is working part time, it is just about possible to 'overlook' this work when constructing an account of relational equality. However, full-time work on the woman's part creates a serious problem for the ideology. I am not trying to suggest here that no alternative forms of division of labour (such as role reversal) exist. Rather, I want to suggest that the women I interviewed were not convinced that it would be a viable option in their marriages. Nevertheless, they were trying to construe their situation as 'fair'. The problem was that structural changes such as full-time work could pose a particular challenge to this tenuous construction.

In this connection, Janet's comment concerning pressure is ambiguous. 'Pressure' could refer to the extra workload that she fears would be involved for her if she took a job. However, she also says she might be 'saying a few different things' to Simon if she was working. In other words, she is anticipating some form of potential conflict here between herself and Simon. She then says she is actually quite glad she did not get the job after all because she doesn't like operating under pressure. Either, therefore, she means that she cannot see Simon unburdening her of some of this extra pressure or she means that conflict with him over this issue would create pressure in itself.

Turning to another example from my interviews, Joanna Hardy originally gave up her job when she had a baby, but the couple were able to afford a nanny and someone to do the housework and Joanna now worked full time, from home, in her own business. The couple also told me that their ambition was for Bernard to come into the business eventually. The following extract is part of a discussion that Joanna, Bernard and I had about role reversal. I had just asked them what they thought about the scenario of a man taking the children to play-school – if they thought this could prove difficult:

JOANNA: It's like, the friend that Bernard was just talking about, who's just sort of swapped roles. When he was here that was one of the examples he used actually. He goes to play-school with his son.

BERNARD: He goes, 'to mother and toddler group' [said in a silly voice].

JOANNA: [ignoring him] And I think that's really great. That's really good. But, I mean, that circumstance...wouldn't arise, because...probably I wouldn't be taking her to play-group. It would be somebody else taking her to play-group [i.e. the nanny].

In this extract, Bernard's derisory humour over the term 'mother and toddler group' suggests to me – and arguably also to Joanna, who ignored him – that going to mother and toddler group is in some way a demeaning thing to do and may provide a problem for Bernard. I will return to the issue of women's role being undervalued in Chapter 3. However, for now, I want to suggest that Joanna hoped she would be able to avoid the potential stigma of the husband doing something like going to mother and toddler group because the nanny could take the child. But more than this, I would argue that Joanna was also using the reference to 'paid help' here as a way out of the potential problem of role conflict between herself and Bernard. In doing so, she was able to preserve an account of fairness, for although the couple were both working, neither of them would have to take the child to play-group when she was old enough because the nanny would do it.

Taking the blame

A third and extremely pervasive way in which women engaged in book balancing was to defuse accounts of conflict by blaming themselves for a particular set of events. This process of self blame has already been touched on above in the extract from Karen Craven (p. 38). Karen used the minimising 'silly daft things' to initiate a cautious challenge of her husband's response to her cooking. However, at the end of the extract above when he comes into the room she says:

KAREN: It's only a stupid thing you know but I think I p'rhaps take things too personally I don't know. I take things to heart [he mumbles 'yeah']. Shut up! [laughing]

She sets the parameters of the debate for herself in the first sentence when she says 'I think sometimes perhaps he's a bit critical...', 'or perhaps I take things too personally'. Which is it? When he comes into the room she laughs and says she thinks she takes things too personally. In other words she blames herself for the argument. In saying that Karen blamed herself for conflict in this extract, I am not suggesting that she consistently blamed herself for their ongoing disagreements. However, I think she blamed herself in this instance to balance the books of fairness in front of me. The important point here is the nature and consequence of the explanation used to do this. Woman blame as an insidious cultural practice has now been extensively documented by feminist writers across the social sciences (e.g. see Billinghurst 1996; Burns and Griffin 1996 for examples of contemporary research on the topic). Karen is here drawing on a discourse already in the public domain that effectively destroys her challenge before it is fully articulated. The act of blaming herself functions to render the account once more equitable, and therefore 'safe', but it lets Will off the hook.

Turning to another example of this process, in the following extract from the separate interview with Gillian Henderson, I have just asked her if she and her husband ever row. She said no, they just had 'little niggles':

GILLIAN: We hardly ever have a row.

CAROLINE: No, I remember you saying that yeah.

GILLIAN: Um [pause] the last time we did actually was last Saturday and it was – it was when I had the flu, and <u>I hadn't realised I had the flu</u>. [pause] I couldn't think why – I don't usually [pause] you know.

CAROLINE: Mm. What did you/

GILLIAN: And I just – I – I shouted at him! and then burst into tears and – suddenly realised I felt absolutely lousy and it wasn't anything to do with him at all [slight laugh]. It was because I felt so ill, and once I went to bed I was alright. I'm hardly ever – actually [pause]

CAROLINE: Right. What was it about at the time? Was it/

GILLIAN: Oh we'd bought a pair of shoes for Mandy and they'd rubbed her heel. And er [pause] I think he said something to the effect of, oh well, if it hasn't got better by Monday you'll have to take them back. [pause] [slight uncertain laugh from me then she laughs]. The – the last thing I wanted to do was to go back to [town] and take these [pause] shoes back. You know but um [pause] 'Its always me!' – you know [pause] <u>which of course it is because I'm here you know which is…perfectly logical. But</u>…

This extract from Gillian is prefaced by the minimising 'little niggles' and the final underlined phrase also highlights the now familiar traditional (practical) construction of fairness. However, the most important feature of this extract is that Gillian begins by saying she hadn't realised that she'd got flu, and in the middle of the extract she completely exonerates Patrick from blame for the argument by saying it wasn't anything to do with him, whilst saying that it was because she felt so ill (all underlined above). In other words, Gillian has blamed herself (her unwell body) in this account for the incident with the shoes, albeit she is not suggesting that she contracted flu on purpose.

In a third example of shouldering the blame, I asked Heather Morris in her one-to-one interview if she and Gerry ever rowed. She said, yes they did, they rowed about little things:

HEATHER: Just little things, little things usually. Usually the untidiness of the place, yes, that – he seems to take so much and then it, you know, he goes back and – and I can fully, you know, appreciate it really. Um [pause] I like to think that the house is clean but it's certainly not tidy, and I think Gerry would like it tidy. Um – and I don't think it's gonna be tidy [I laugh a bit]. Um [pause] and I feel I ought to change, I'd like to be tidy! but, um [pause] [she shrugs and we both laugh]. Takes too long. Perhaps I ought to stop being a hoarder, that would help.

Here we see, once again, the 'it's little things' followed by an account of conflict (which Gerry also relates to me as being an issue in his separate interview). At this stage Heather blames herself for the conflict – she simply 'can't' keep the house tidy, although she would like to. However, in this particular interview I then actually asked Heather what her side of this was:

CAROLINE: What's your side of that, when you have a row, what – what point of view do you put?

HEATHER: Well, that I, I'm a childminder. I do quite a, um, I don't earn very much because the – the childminder's pay's dreadful. [pause] And, I also work at the play-group. So I think well I'm not here, a great deal, and when I am here, I've got more than one child. So e– it's time – it comes down to, that you know, I haven't really got the time to do it all.

So here we have quite a different picture from Heather, who – with some prompting from me – now mentions her childminding and play-group duties and her severe lack of time. (She is also a school governor and does some other work on the side!) However, before I could say anything else, Heather continued the above passage with:

HEATHER: But…it's not much of an excuse really, cause an awful lot of people work full time and keep their house tidy as well [slight laugh]. I don't know how.

In sum, prefacing or concluding accounts of conflict with the suggestion that the whole thing was probably her fault anyway was a pervasive theme amongst the women I interviewed. In saying this, I am *not* saying that the women in my sample appeared to display some 'pre-disposition to blame themselves' for marital conflict. On the contrary, in all the interviews referred to above there was evidence that women were able to articulate the problem in different ways that did not necessarily involve self-blame, as Heather does here when prompted by me. I think in part that the obligation to construct the relationship as already equal within the interview situation acted here as a bit of a straight-jacket to women and probably encouraged this book-balancing process. On the other hand, the interviews also gave women the chance to discuss these issues and their recounting of discussions with their husbands suggested a rather tenacious quality to this type of book balancing in the women's relationships. I will return to this point shortly but, for now, I want to move on to examine briefly the fourth book-balancing practice that I identified in my interviews.

Making positive comparisons

The fourth pattern of book balancing I want to examine involved a comparative process that incorporated an aspect of distancing discussed at the beginning of this section. In the same way that women were often careful to criticise or challenge in a depersonalised or hypothetical way, thereby protecting their own husband from direct criticism, women also frequently made favourable comparisons at various points in the interviews between their own husbands and other people's. Essentially, then, this process involved a woman suggesting that she was really quite lucky because her husband was 'much better than most' – or most husbands appeared to be worse than hers. Comments such as the following were common:

GILLIAN: I hear other women, they tell these awful stories, you know. [pause] [whispering] 'I haven't made the bed. I had to rush home', you know. These are women who are out at work – 'I had to rush home and get – try and get the bed made before he came home. And he got there first and he...' [me laughing]. It's terrible and if he said that to me I'd say – well you make it, you know, but

CAROL: I wouldn't like him to tell me, you know, you're gonna do the washing today and you're gonna do the vacuuming today, you know. I couldn't stand that. No. But I mean I know a couple of women that – gotta get all their housework done before their husbands get home.

AMANDA: And other marriages I've seen, well I – you know, I thi– [pause] w– lots of them seem to – when I'm just down the mother and toddlers and talking, you know. They're not, they're not ecstatically happy with their husbands and that you know. And the husbands don't seem to um [pause] do very much, you know, sort of, to be equal partners. They're not as equal partners you know so um.

These kinds of positive comparisons were usually of the 'there's a lot worse than he is' variety. In other words, they are actually positive comparisons around a negative. When I first identified this kind of comparative theme in the women's interview data it reminded me of a comment that an elderly friend, now in her late seventies, had made to me some years ago when she said that she had been lucky in her marriage in comparison with a lot of women. At least he never hit her.

Internal debates at the crossroads

At this juncture, I want to make the point that challenges to the status quo of a relationship could in some sense be seen as indicative of a rather more general practice that women frequently engaged in throughout the interviews. I think women were often taking up the possibility presented in the interview to have a debate with themselves about just exactly what the status of their relationship really was. In having this debate, I think, they were invariably moving backwards and forwards at the metaphorical crossroads (outlined in Chapter 1) between the contradictory elements of intergroup and interpersonal. In order to demonstrate what I mean here, I want to use two further examples of conflict from my interviews. These examples also illustrate in broader context something of the positive comparison process I have discussed above.

Example 1

Margaret and Richard Price appeared to have quite a lot of problems in their relationship during the period spanned by both sets of interviews. Their presentation of their relationship was particularly contradictory. Both, at different times, were keen to present their marriage as stable and equitable. However, the interviews taken as a whole indicated that the couple had been experiencing considerable emotional difficulties. This was particularly evident at the separate interviews when Richard was, by this stage, seeing the local doctor about what was described to me as 'the problem of his temper'. One of the biggest differences of opinion in Richard and Margaret's relationship, gleaned mainly from the joint interview and Richard's separate interview was that Richard did not feel he 'was allowed out' enough with his friends or for his hobbies. So, for example:

RICHARD: Can't remember what brought it on I, I [pause] – pretty naffed off really, that um, I wasn't…everybody else seemed to be going off doing their thing and, I just wasn't really able to.

MARGARET: Who's everybody else then?

RICHARD: Well all my friends seemed to be doing this and that, and I had to sort of beg permission, well, how it felt [pause] to get an hour out, away from the house with the– and it was – well alright, but what about so and so, you haven't done so and so, and you haven't done this and that. And [pause] Margaret's argument was that I had to do the jobs, I felt like the argument was I had to do the jobs and my reward was an escape for five minutes. Now that got up my nose. And, I saw it the other way, that if I was allowed to do something then I would feel more willing to do something in the house or in the garden. And that really is, um, how it came about. But you know, I was totally fed up. And there didn't seem to be [pause] well, cheesed right off, didn't seem to be any point doing anything cause I wasn't [pause] you know,

what was the point. I couldn't go out and do anything so I wasn't gonna do anything in here. Wasn't quite like that, but um, you know, pretty angry.
[and then again:]

RICHARD: Most people seem to me to be able to get out, away from their wives and families, certainly my friends do – that includes Bill and um Dave...
[and then again in my separate interview with Richard:]

RICHARD: I don't quite go out as often as I like. I don't do too badly. No doubt she'll tell you I go out far too often but...

Richard also told me in his separate interview that he sometimes 'pops out for a drink with the lads and tells fibs about the time they get back'.

It is interesting to note in the above extract that Richard appears to be blaming Margaret for his particular set of problems, and I will return to this point in Chapter 4. At this stage, however, I want to focus on the point that, set in the context of these two other interviews, the whole of Margaret's separate interview with me seems to be taken up with a kind of debate with me *and herself* over the meaning of Richard's behaviour in relation to her. But this is cautiously done. At one stage she talked about how they 'had to sort out' the fact that he wasn't 'getting out as much as he should' so he now goes out one day a month on his hobby. However, towards the end of the interview, the following conversation ensues:

MARGARET: I think, in a lot of marriages, probably, only from, you know, the divorce statistics and er, you know, the – the amount that you hear that the husband's down the pub five nights a week – if you're content with your home life, um, I – I, I can't imagine why people – go to have affairs or – why the man – mean it's not only the man is it, the wife as well. Um – or the man goes down the pub. They're obviously not getting, what they consider the ideal from their marriage are they?

Arguably, what is happening here is that Margaret is airing a concern that is close to her heart and, in a sense, trying to talk it through with me to make sense of it and asking for my view. In doing this, however, she is careful to take an extreme example ('down the pub five nights a week') and talk in general terms and, in so doing, she is distancing her own relationship from her concern. She apparently only knows about these problems from the divorce statistics and from what 'you hear' about husbands being down the pub. She can't imagine why men would want to do this. They can't be getting enough from their marriage – can they?

I found this conversation very difficult at the time. I felt that if I agreed with Margaret it would be insensitive because I would be implying that her husband did not get enough from their marriage. In the event, rightly or wrongly, I did not answer her question but instead reflected it back to her. The conversation continued as follows:

MARGARET: Do you see what I mean?

CAROLINE: So you think that er – the reason why a m– a man might go down the pub a lot is because they're not happy?

MARGARET: Yes. I mean if, if er [pause] you know, if they were content at home, to find something to do together or – um – just be happy with each other's company or whatever, they – they wouldn't feel the need to um, you know, if – Richard'll sometimes say 'Oh I fancy a quick pint' and then he'll say five minutes later, ohh no, I'll stay here. He's, he's happy to sort of stay here, whereas a lot of men can't wait till they're – sort of 8 o'clock 'Oh right I'm off' – off down the pub. They're obviously – something…[she tails off here].

After I put the question back to Margaret she continues talking hypothetically but then she explicitly brings her own husband into the frame and makes a positive comparison between Richard and hypothetical men who go down the pub. Margaret, by distancing Richard from this type of behaviour, seems to be trying to separate the images that she has brought together a moment before and thus balance the books. In the context of the other discussions with the couple together and with Richard separately, I found Margaret's account very sad.

Margaret's position seemed particularly sad given the severity of the difficulties she and her husband discussed with me (and I will be returning to this couple's problems later in the book). As I have stated above, their relationship was overtly unstable and both spouses presented me with many contradictory statements during the interviews. However, Margaret's position was typical in my sample in the sense that, as the major caregiver of young children and with the major household wage coming from her husband's employment, she was economically dependent on her spouse as were all of the women in my study to a greater or lesser extent. Debates about the status of the relationship were therefore being conducted by women on an uneven economic playing field. This economic dependency would be likely to restrict severely the realistic choices that these women could make about their lives and, in fact, a number of feminist writers (e.g. Barrett and Mackintosh 1982) have characterised a woman's decision to marry in the first place as often a sensible choice given the restricted set of alternative options available to them. I think, therefore, that there were clear practical reasons why the women I interviewed would want to be able to make sense of their relationship *as fair* and why women would quite often reason that their own husband was better than other men. (Perhaps a case of the 'devil you know'?) If most men are worse than yours and independent living is out of the question (or too frightening), you might as well make the best of it. However, I think Margaret's extract above also illustrates the point that marriages are about more than practical considerations. In Margaret's case at least, there were likely to be strong emotional as well as practical reasons for such a positive comparison process.

A major aspect of Margaret's internal debate throughout her separate interview with me was essentially: 'How can Richard really love me if he wants to go out all the time and doesn't want to be with me?' Her attempt to make sense of these kinds of issues throughout her interview highlights an important point related to the construction of relational identity. In the traditional 'fairy-tale' or Mills and Boon account of perfect heterosexual love, the man is often cast as highly chauvinistic in his life relations generally. However, he meets the right woman and their love transcends the problem of chauvinism. She is immune from his oppressive practices through his strong romantic identification with her. Margaret's husband should not be behaving like a chauvinist man *to her* because through relational identification she should have become his equal. Heterosexual love should span the murky water of the relational crossroads (and see Ussher 1997 for a more detailed discussion of romantic love and power).

The second example of the theme of internal argument, and also related to a process of positive comparison, is taken from the interviews with Joan and Peter Docherty.

Example 2

Joan and Peter also discussed problems in their relationship with me and a particular problematic theme involves the children. This account is taken from a separate interview with Joan Docherty. I had just asked Joan if she felt she cared enough for Peter (a question I asked everyone). She told me that she has her moments when she doesn't care about him at all – but overall, really, she feels that she couldn't care more than she does already. I asked her what moments she is referring to when she feels she doesn't care at all:

JOAN: Um [longish pause] I find it difficult sometimes – again it conflicts with the children I suppose in that they need me at certain times and if he wants me there as well, then I think 'oh for goodness sake!' you know – go away I don't – It's more – it's quite often in the evening sort of, bedtime, not, not our bedtime, their bedtime. And if I've got them [longish pause] ready for bed and sort of quietened down, and then he arrives home and there's all hell let loose again [sighing] [pause] – 'can't you just have stayed out for half – half an hour and they'd have been in bed and asleep it <u>it's just silly things like that it's nothing big.</u> Just at time it's sort of [pause] all too – you know you kind of pull yourself in too many directions.

In this extract the minimising 'it's silly things' belies the seriousness of the problem. In all three interviews with the Dochertys, both Joan and Peter told me at different times and in different ways that Peter is not particularly fond of children. In fact he told me he now wishes they didn't have children, although they were both in agreement about having them in the first place. Self-confessedly, he has virtually nothing to do with child-care and this is clearly an ongoing source of conflict between the couple.

In a continuation of the above account by Joan, I would argue that it becomes very clear that what Joan is doing is having an internal debate (through me) over the status of Peter's behaviour. Is it fair or unfair?

JOAN: I – I cause I said to him a while ago, cause he was talking about getting home at – various times, cause he often doesn't get in till about half past six, and I said, to be honest I'd rather he was either here at 5 o'clock or half past 5 or didn't come home till about half past 7. [I laugh slightly.] That half past 6 is just the wrong time – for me – or for us. Er, if I know, he's not coming in till later, I – I'm much calmer, and I can get them into bed, and I don't keep thinking oh, I'd like to be downstairs talking to him or I'd like to be getting supper or something. Um [pause] so then I get cross with them cause they won't settle down – and I want to be down here doing the supper – although he quite often does it but – you know. If I just know he's not coming in till late then I'm much calmer with them and get them all settled and it all seems to go much easier. Or else if he's here earlier and we've got over all that excitement of him coming home [pause].

CAROLINE: Do you feel, he does enough with the children?

JOAN: [pause] No. Not really.

CAROLINE: W– why do you think that is?

JOAN: [pause] [she laughs] He doesn't like children – um [I laugh.]. No [as in no, seriously]. He's not very good with young children. He gets [pause] he finds [pause] e– he's finding Rebecca easier now cause she's more – interesting, more interested in other things. Um, but he still finds Stephen quite difficult I think. Um, and Philip's a bit of a Mummy's boy really. Mummy's boy. Um [pause] I think [pause] he f– I mean he gets tired as well, and then he comes home and I expect him to play games with the kids and he doesn't – he – I don't think he really enjoys young children. He's getting better with them as they're getting older, and I think when they're big enough to take round museums and – show things and do things – he gets a bit fed up with the moaning and the whining and he does expect that what he says is done, 'like that' [clicking fingers] you know. And it isn't. Its got to be, you know – I'm used to saying everything a hundred times.

CAROLINE: Mm.

JOAN: Um [pause] he rather expects his word to be law sometimes and they just don't [longish pause] don't want to know.

CAROLINE: Yeah, right.

JOAN: Er, I – er – yes, I do wish he would do more. Quite often on a weekend, you know, we'll have lunch and he'll come in here and – doze off on the settee and then I get cross about it. – I can't do that! you know [laughing] Um – but I mean I know he's tired from work as well so I shouldn't blame him really but – at times you think [almost under breath] coh! you know – he could do a bit more. Make, make a bit more of an effort. And yet at other times he's fine, you know.

So, having asserted earlier in the conversation that this is only a 'little thing', Joan goes on to have quite a lengthy debate with herself (and possibly me) over the status of Peter's behaviour. First, she suggests that the problem with the timing of his homecoming is that it makes work for her – but then she qualifies this with – 'although he often does the supper'. Then I ask if she feels he does enough with the children and she says 'no, not really'. She says he doesn't like/isn't very good with children, but then qualifies this by saying that he comes home tired and she expects him to play with them. In the last paragraph above she goes from – 'he doesn't do enough' to – 'I wish he would do more' – to – 'I know he's tired/and yet at times he's fine'. In fact, I would argue that virtually the whole of Joan's one-to-one interview with me can be seen in some sense as an internal debate around Peter's behaviour. However, as much as possible, she keeps within the confines of an overall account of fairness, although in the above extract the final comment that 'at other times he's fine' seems a bit lame.

Towards the end of her separate interview with me, Joan told me that she thought traditional marriage was changing – most wives tend to go back to work:

JOAN: And um – the husbands often do a lot more. At home or with the children. Not in every case as I say. One couple who – he just isn't terribly interested at all in the children, he just goes off and does what he wants.

CAROLINE: How does she cope with that then?

JOAN: Oh she's amazing. You know, three girls – I often wonder if she'd – if he'd had a boy – if it would have been different. But he's just not very interested in family life at all. She just gets on with it. Poor thing.

Aside from the suggestion in the above that this 'other husband' might have been more interested had the child been a boy, Joan, in this extract, as with Margaret earlier, draws on a subject matter that seems close to her heart but discusses it in a way that is distanced from her own relationship. When she talks about a husband who does not do much with his children, this husband is not her own. On the contrary, by saying 'poor thing' at the end of this extract she is, by implication, favourably comparing her own life (and husband) with her friend's. Again I found this conversation with Joan very sad. As with Margaret, above, the sadness is that the tale seemed to so closely describe her own situation. Again, I think the sub-text of the discussion for Joan was 'how can Peter love me and the children if he cuts himself off from us in this way?'

To summarise this section, I have used these two examples above to try to illustrate something of the way in which I think women's cautious challenges to the status quo of their relationship often formed part of a broader internal debate. Interviews made it possible for women to rehearse and explore aspects of this debate with and through me. At the same time, the outcome of this debate was heavily influenced by a social obligation to construct the relationship as equal and the attendant problems involved in not accomplishing this. I have used

Margaret and Joan's extracts above to try to show that failing to accomplish a construction of relational equality could be highly *problematic* for the woman. That is, by openly admitting the inequality of their relationships, they would cause themselves embarrassment in front of me and also exacerbate their personal distress.

In emphasising the importance of viewing women's conversations as a form of debate, I also want to make the point that whilst *cautious* challenge was extremely common within my interviews with the women, there were, nevertheless, some isolated occasions, notably in joint interviews, when women seemed to throw caution to the wind and launch what seemed to be a more open challenge to the status quo of their relationship. It is also important to underline the point here that it was not necessarily the simple case that some women challenged cautiously whilst some challenged directly. I want to expand on this in the next section of the chapter.

Open challenges

In order to illustrate what I mean by open challenge whilst simultaneously making the point that one woman might use both cautious and direct approaches at different times, I want to continue by looking at data from Joan, this time with her husband in their joint interview.

We join the conversation where she has been talking about the difficulty of switching from mother to wife in the evenings and at weekends. Here again, Joan seems to be having a debate, but this time it is with her husband rather than with herself.

JOAN: But [pause] over the weekends I do, I resent it sometimes, on a Sunday I must admit. I sometimes think 'ohh' you know. I really [pause] quite resent the fact that I can't just sit quietly and, you know, um [pause] that it should be my day off as well and it isn't! you know [laughing a bit].

Peter did not reply to Joan's comment, which was patently directed at his not doing any work on a Sunday. I changed the subject at this stage in the interview. Then, later on in the interview, I asked if the couple were planning to have any more children:

JOAN: [pause] No [quietly].
PETER: No. No more [firmly].
JOAN: He definitely doesn't want any more [laughs].
CAROLINE: Would you be tempted then?
PETER: [laughing] She'd carry on having them till/
JOAN: Um. I think if I had a husband who was desperate for more children I wouldn't say no, but then one assumes that if he was desperate for more

children he'd be marvellous with children and – and, you know, spend his whole Saturdays and Sundays playing with them so it would be easier.

CAROLINE: Mm. Right.

JOAN: Not that you don't play with them but [pause] you know, some husbands absolutely dote on the – I mean <u>I've got one friend who's got three children and the youngest is still not 4. And the husband – you know he absolutely dotes on them. I mean, just spends his whole time when he's home playing with them</u>. Um.
[pause]

PETER: No, I'm a bit selfish really I s'pose.

JOAN: But no I think, you know, we're happy as we are. It's fine. So if you definitely don't want any more, that's fair enough.

In this extract then, once again the topic is a father's role with the children. It is interesting here that towards the end of the extract Joan uses a comparative device, as she did in the separate interview when she said Peter was much better than other men who don't play with their children. This time however, she openly challenges Peter and suggests he is much *worse* than a friend's husband who dotes on his children. This variation in the use of a comparative device highlights the flexible nature of such categorisations and underlines Potter and Wetherell's (1987) point that we need to understand language in terms of its functions rather than just assuming that people's comments will easily reflect an internal stable attitude or perception. In openly challenging Peter in this way, Joan arguably creates a situation in which he becomes relationally accountable in front of me. It is also interesting to note in the above example, however, that when Peter suggested that 'I might be a bit selfish really I s'pose', Joan immediately reconstructed equity by saying they were 'fine' as they were; there was no problem – as though his sudden humility and (not altogether convincing) suggestion that he might be at fault jolts her into stepping back from the brink of this open challenge. In other words, her challenge was not sustained.

In fact, I think Joan's open challenge to Peter above can still best be seen as part of an overall debate she is having with herself and, at this point, with Peter, concerning the status of their relationship. There were one or two other moments in joint interviews where women instigated open challenges to their husbands around the status quo of the relationship and, again, these open challenges could usually best be understood in terms of an overall debate or argument (either with self or spouse, with or through me). For example, in the case of Sally and Nick Freeman. Throughout both interviews with the couple Sally seemed stressed and her comments often seemed particularly contradictory. When I arrived at the Freemans' house for the second interview, she seemed particularly harrassed. She asked if I minded her ironing during the interview and, when we commenced, she set off at a frenetic pace to tackle an enormous black sack full of the family's clothes. The atmosphere appeared very tense:

CAROLINE: Do you think, in any ways, your relationship's changed over the last – getting on for two years?

[She's looking at him.]

CAROLINE: Can [I ask? [laughing slightly]

SALLY: [I don't think so really do you?

NICK: [pause] Mm, not really. Um [long pause].

SALLY : [rummaging around in plastic bag of ironing] I don't usually do the ir– I don't usually do all the ironing [I laugh and the atmosphere seems to break a bit.]

CAROLINE: Right.

SALLY: We do share things [laughing a bit]. I – no I don't actually think our relationship has changed actually, do you?

NICK: Mm, no.

In the above extract, Sally seemed to be attempting a construction of relational equality by saying that they share things and that she doesn't usually do all the ironing. However, her body language contradicted her comments. She seemed extremely tense and, as the interview progressed, Sally continued to iron in an extremely 'obvious' sort of way. She seemed to fluctuate between being very agitated, calming down, and then becoming agitated again. She spent a lot of time looking at Nick before she answered questions and he was quite reticent at certain points. Once or twice they seemed to be on the brink of an open row, for example, about money. Nick told me 'I let her get away with' spending money – whereupon Sally immediately challenged this construction by asking him what exactly he meant by such a statement.

The interview was also punctuated with Sally saying things like:

SALLY: I – I, I sometimes sort of have this dream of sort of going away somewhere and not having to wash up

[to which Nick retorts]

NICK: Alone! [I laugh awkwardly but she doesn't.]

They also argued in front of me about home maintenance – with Sally implying that, although this is Nick's sphere of responsibility, he has not done any recently. Then, at one point in the interview, Sally interjects with:

SALLY: Can you iron your own trousers?

NICK: Yeah.

CAROLINE: Sorry? [I hadn't heard.]

SALLY: I can – I can never iron trousers. He has to do his own trousers. [I laugh a bit – she doesn't.]

[And then, towards the end of the interview, I ask:]

CAROLINE: Do you think that um – marriage has er – thinking about roles in marriage, do you think that's changed over the last say, ten years?

SALLY: What, with me standing up doing the ironing and him sitting? [I laugh alone.]

Finally, at the end of the interview, Sally moved from doing the ironing and picked up an enormous sewing box to do the mending. She commented that she supposed 'he could have done the mending couldn't he'. Nick did not answer.

I will be talking more about Sally and Nick's relationship in Chapter 4, but here I want to make the point that I believe Sally was actually using the ironing as a way of trying to put across her position to Nick and using the interview and me as a vehicle to do this. I would also point out that the technique Sally was using above was not just verbal and I will return to this issue later in the book. As can be seen from the above, she progressed from saying at the beginning of the interview that she did not usually do the ironing, to saying towards the end concerning role change 'what, with me doing the ironing and him sitting?' In fact, I would argue that the whole of this joint interview could be construed as an argument that Sally was having with Nick where she seemed to fluctuate continually between getting cross with him and calming down again. It is also interesting to note that throughout the whole of the couple's interviews Nick keeps very quiet. I will come back to this point in Chapter 5.

Although I think there was a strong element of open challenge to Nick in the above extracts with the Freemans, the fluctuations across the interview and the fact that much of the time her challenges were non-verbal meant that, in the interview taken as a whole, the overall effect was still muted. There was, in fact, only one woman in my study who came close to sustaining an open challenge to her husband throughout the interviews taken as a whole and that was Cathy Thompson. Cathy and Brian Thompson's joint interview was peppered with open disagreement and 'bickering'. Although both Cathy and Brian did draw on overall statements of fairness around the traditional division of labour – the major organising principle here being the traditional homemaker/breadwinner ideology – Cathy, in her joint and separate interviews, openly complained in places about her gendered position. She said she felt she was not 'cut out' to be a mother and had very much enjoyed going back to work part time (although she said at one point that she worried sometimes about women taking men's jobs). Brian was a keen sportsperson and he also, by his own admission, liked a drink in the pub 'with the lads'. I was told that he went out quite a lot on his own, either playing cricket or football, or drinking. Over the years, this had caused considerable friction, both spouses told me, although Cathy said she was finally becoming resigned to the situation:

CAROLINE: What about um, actually, you know, who does what in terms of everyday things? Do you have a kind of rota or do you – how do you divide up what you do?

CATHY: [laughing sarcastically] [We don't, I do it all.

BRIAN: [laughing sarcastically] [Sort of – I well, weekends, weekends I tend to do more don't I?

CATHY: Yeah, oh yeah. He gets the children up and – b/

BRIAN: I used to, I must admit I am get– I think I, I am a bit lazy, I haven't been doing as much/

CATHY: Male – male chauvinist

BRIAN: [tongue in cheek] But I've been working so much harder in work dear.

CATHY: He thinks I was put on this earth to serve him.

BRIAN: No I don't! [laughing a bit awkwardly] No, that's a bit strong in't it? [I laugh awkwardly – she doesn't.]

CAROLINE: Do you have any…do you have any disagreements about it or?

CATHY: No…sometimes.

BRIAN: Only minor ones though, nothing…nothing big.

CAROLINE: What do you, what kind of things do you expect, or would you like?

CATHY: Um [pause]

BRIAN: Me to finish the decorating?

CATHY: Yeah.

BRIAN: [laughing]

CATHY: What else. Um [pause] I don't know. [to self] What is it? I'd like him to do the gardening.

BRIAN: I'm not keen on gardening. I keep getting these mad, mad rushes, and think ah yes I'll go out and do it, and I'm cutting some rose bushes and then by that – by that time, all the weeds are grown back again. So I'm not keen on gardening. No, I, I'm the same with decorating. I get a – a mad idea that I [wanna do some decorating.

CATHY: [Yes. That's the same as everybody [laughing] [or nearly everybody.

BRIAN: [Yeah.

[more regarding the practicalities of decorating]

CAROLINE: But do you – what about things like cooking and cleaning/

BRIAN: I do cook, sometimes don't I?

CATHY: Oh – you can only cook one thing though.

BRIAN: What?!

CATHY: Fish cakes.

BRIAN: No I can [cook – toasted sandwiches.

CATHY: [and chips. Oh yeah – you did make me one last week.

BRIAN: I do – well I do do the kids' fairly often, when you're not around.

CATHY: Yeah.

BRIAN: If you go down town and what have you. And I've cooked yours before now as well – on quite a few occasions really [atmosphere getting quite tense here].

CATHY: Not as many occasions as I cook yours.

BRIAN: No I mean I obviously, I could, I probably could do it more, but obviously, coming home from work [pause] it's too late really, for me to do it, if you know what I mean.

CATHY: Yeah, I s'pose so. Mm.

At the end of this extract, it is Brian who draws on the traditional (practical) claim to fairness. Cathy replied 'yes I s'pose so, mm' but sounded unconvinced and the atmosphere by then had become quite tense. Although Brian made a couple of attempts at jokes throughout this exchange, Cathy was mostly serious and quite accusational throughout the exchange. It was obvious from other comments in their interviews that the couple had had open disagreements at some level about women's position in society, and the equality or otherwise of their relationship. For example, in the separate interview with Cathy:

CAROLINE: So do you talk about that sort of thing to him or?
CATHY: He says [said very deliberately] – that women should be equal. But having said that, his attitude is going along in a very old fashioned – thing.
CAROLINE: Right.
CATHY: He'll still believe that I should wait on him and, you know, stuff like that.

The major point here is that Cathy was making no attempt in these two extracts to present Brian to me as a liberated man. In fact, in the joint extract, Brian appeared to be struggling to some extent to counterbalance Cathy's impression and present a more liberal picture. In line 17 (underlined), it is interesting to note that it was Brian who supplied the minimising 'it's little things', not Cathy. Brian, I would argue, was the one here who was superficially working quite hard to create a semblance of fairness. In fact, I will be arguing in Chapter 4 that I don't think Brian was totally wholehearted in this attempt at managing fairness across their interviews. What is more, his apparent shouldering of some blame by saying he might be a bit lazy in this extract does not have the same identity implications as women's expressions of self-blame discussed earlier. I will explain what I mean here in Chapter 4. But for now, the major point I want to make is that Cathy, by refusing to pass Brian off as a 'liberated man' and by openly challenging him in front of me, was drawing attention to a potential power imbalance in their relationship and calling him to account for this.

Summary

Drawing my arguments together, I emphasised in Chapter 1 that I think couples experienced social pressure to construct relational equality when talking to me in the interviews. However, I have also emphasised in this chapter that the interview situation provided the possibility for women to use me to have a debate with themselves and, if they got the chance, a debate with their husbands, concerning the fairness or otherwise of their relationship using discussions of division of household labour as a vehicle for this. Challenges to the status quo of a marriage often emerged from these debates – most cautious and a few not so cautious. I have given examples above of the more open challenges as they occurred in the interviews. Even here, however, taken in the context of the interview as a whole, open challenges were rarely sustained. When challenges became too overt, women frequently engaged in 'book-balancing' practices to reconstruct relational equality. A particularly insidious form of book balancing involved self-blame. I have tried to show in this chapter that I believe women's engagement in book-balancing strategies such as self-blame in order to make sense of the relationship as fair or equal were rarely just for me. Rather, the speaker was often trying to create a semblance of balance *for themselves.*

The sustained practice of self-blame for problems such as those discussed in this chapter would be unlikely to help women construct for themselves a positive self-image. However, before I make the mistake of appearing to 'blame women for blaming themselves' in such situations, I need to underline two further points.

The interviews highlighted that women were frequently in 'Catch 22' situations. Restricted economic and related practical choices would make some constructions of reality difficult to act upon. For example, a woman's husband is supposed to be her closest adult companion. The marital relationship is supposed to be about intimacy, love, sharing and close personal identification. This close personal identification *should* transcend social inequalities of any kind. An acknowledgement that this might not be the case is likely to be stressful at any time. At a time when there are severely restricted practical life options available (i.e. young children and financial dependence), such an acknowledgement might be emotionally almost too hard to bear. Cathy, in the last extract reproduced above, openly challenged her husband at various times in the interview but there was an element of resignation in her challenge. With two young children, highly restricted potential earning capacity for self and a husband who was showing no sign of wanting to change, what were the realistic options for Cathy? A daily 'realisation' that your husband is behaving in a 'chauvinistic' way is a 'realisation' that someone in Cathy's position may not be able to do much with. In this analysis, self-blame starts to look like an eminently sensible strategy for traversing an emotional minefield – or dealing with the murky territory that is the marital 'crossroads'.

There was significant evidence in my interviews that all the women *were able to* articulate alternative versions of events that did not involve self-blame. Interviews were full of challenges and, despite the social obligations of the situation, some of these challenges were quite explicit. In fact, all of the women I interviewed were at some level within the interview actively challenging inequalities in their relationships and trying to 'meaning make' in a different way. In this sense, women's accounts could be seen as forming part of a challenge to unequal gender power relations. The extracts reproduced above of open challenge demonstrate potential problems for husbands in this regard and perhaps represent the impact of feminism on these women's lives. In sacrificing relational accountability for challenge, wives were effectively calling their husbands to account as individuals. Peter Docherty actually suggested he might be a bit selfish following his wife's challenge; Brian Thompson, we saw above, tried in that particular extract to balance his wife's account with a 'fair' one. Nick was very quiet throughout both sets of interviews.

Bearing these final two points in mind – and in order to continue my investigation of interrelated processes of marital identity, gender power relations and emotional experience – in the next chapter I go on to explore the sub-text of what men were doing when they talked about division of labour in their marriages. In doing this, I will be looking at the phenomenon of 'woman blame' from a different angle.

4

HUSBANDS AND THE STRUGGLE TO DEFEND RELATIONAL INEQUALITY

> If the world were a computer and somewhere in its control panels, there were a little box marked: 'Default mode for domestic work', what would be written in that box? 'Whoever is free at the time'? Or: 'Whoever's turn it is'? No fear. We all know what it says: 'The bird.'
>
> (Louisa Young, *The Guardian* 9 September 1997)

In this chapter I will focus on how men talked about division of labour in the interviews in the light of my discussion of women's accounts in the last chapter. I have just argued that women were concerned about potential inequalities in their relationships and were using the interviews to try to make challenges to perceived imbalances. However, challenges were muted by various practical and emotional constraints on women and women tended to engage in various book-balancing practices if challenges appeared to go 'too far'. I also said that one pervasive way in which women 'balanced the book of fairness' if discussions of conflict got out of hand was to blame themselves for problems. For example, Karen Craven said that one thing she found difficult was that Will was quite critical of the way she ran the house. However, she told this story and then suggested that the real problem might be that she was too sensitive. Heather Morris referred to conflict that she and Gerry had over her not keeping the house tidy. After prompting by me, she said that when they rowed about this she argued that it was difficult for her to do it because of the childminding, the play-group work and the normal child-care and housework duties. However, she concluded by telling me that 'it's not much of an excuse really'; other people managed and it must be her fault because she was not organised enough. Gillian Henderson told me that she and Patrick never row, but they had had an argument on the previous Saturday about taking some shoes back to a shop. She wanted to know why it should always be her who had to do this sort of thing. However, she quickly realised that the reason why they had had the row was because she had contracted flu; it was nothing to do with Patrick at all. I want to argue in this chapter that not only did wives blame themselves in interviews as a way of reaffirming fairness, but their husbands blamed wives as well. This means that husbands were continually reflecting back negative images of their wives *to their wives.* I am not saying here that this was necessarily part of a conscious attempt by husbands to undermine their wives. In feeding back negative views they were only drawing on explanations that are part of a discourse of woman-blame *already in the public domain* and having considerable common currency. However, they *were* tailoring these types of woman-blaming practices to personally apply to their wives and the overall effect of this negative feedback is unlikely to have been self-esteem bolstering for their wives. In what follows, I will attempt to unravel key aspects of this subtle undermining process.

I believe that interviews created more problems than possibilities for the men in my study. In particular, as we saw in the previous chapter, the interview created a forum for women to have discussions that husbands clearly would often rather not have had. Although most of the men were courteous and hospitable to me, and some seemed genuinely interested to talk, as a group they were less enthusiastic participants than the women – some taking more of a 'back seat' and two, in particular, behaving in quite an antagonistic manner. I think interviews acted to make it hard for men to avoid discussions of some issues that they would rather have avoided, and that their wives were clearly keen to discuss. In fact, interviews provided strong evidence that, where women were challenging, questioning and wanting to make changes to the existing status quo of a relationship, men were metaphoricially 'digging their heels in' and resisting change. However, husbands as well as wives were constrained by social obligations within the interview situation. In short, a major problem created by the interviews for men seemed to be to fend off wives' challenges to the status quo whilst simultaneously accounting for their relationships to their wives (and me) as based on democratic principles, thereby fulfilling a social obligation to construct relational equality. To borrow an expression from the classic sociological work of Bell and Newby (1976), I think the men had a bit of a 'tension managing problem' on their hands.[1]

In this chapter I will identify a number of conversational practices that men engaged in that had the potential to mask the existence of gender inequalities in a marriage through locating the blame for any perceived inequalities in the personality (or biology) of the wife. Specifically, I will be arguing in the following pages that this overall effect of woman-blame could be achieved by: (1) constructing a wife as personally inadequate; (2) constructing the wife's role as biologically given; (3) constructing the self as more than adequate.

Rather like the seeping effect of a dripping tap, I will be arguing that men *personally engaging in these processes* was likely to have been experienced as emotionally disempowering for wives – and in particular is likely to have exacerbated feelings of lack of confidence and guilt amongst wives. It is also worth pointing out that women did not engage in these processes in reverse. Even the open challenges discussed in the previous chapter were not capable of undermining husbands' self-esteem or causing emotional distress in this way (and I will return to this point in Chapter 5).

Constructing a wife as personally inadequate

In this first section, I have identified four conversational practices engaged in by men in the interviews (usually related to the role of housewife and mother) that had the potential to undermine wives' self-esteem and implicitly blame them for any perceived inequalities in existing division-of-labour arrangements.

My 'put-upon' wife

The first theme I identified in husbands' conversations about their wives involved the notion that she could rather easily be 'put upon' by other people. In talking about the fact that the women I interviewed retained major responsibility for housework and child-care it is important to point out at this stage that these women were clearly responsible for caring in a broader sense than just caring for children. This finding resonates with much of the previous sociological literature on family obligations and caring (see Mason 1996 for a review). First of all, it was also clear from my interview data that, next to caring for the children, the biggest caring duty for the wife was caring for the husband. In two cases in particular, that of the Morrises and the Dochertys, the husbands in these relationships by both spouses' account had virtually nothing to do with child-care and took little interest in their children. Both Heather Morris and Joan Docherty suggested at various points in their separate interviews that 'the problem' might sometimes be linked to the fact that they had been unable to give their husbands quite so much attention after the birth of their babies than when the couple were without children. The husbands were probably jealous and Peter Docherty told me at one point that he saw himself more as a husband than a father.

In this connection, some of the men I interviewed were either rather reticent, or sometimes even overtly critical, about aspects of their wives' behaviour related to caring for others. In particular, a common theme in husbands' dialogue involved the notion that wives tended to allow themselves to be 'put upon' rather too much, and this 'being put upon' was construed as a flaw, rather than a virtue.

In the following example from the joint interview with the Hendersons, Patrick (in an account that seems unlikely to bolster Gillian's self-esteem) constructs caring as a flaw and implies that Gillian is rather weak for allowing herself to be 'put upon' by his parents:

PATRICK: Er it does, it came to a head with my parents after we had Stella because [pause] as Gillian said they weren't – they came to visit us once every few months before the baby. And then it got more and more often and then er, one week they came down for a holiday in [town nearby] – and they

just took to dropping in every morning and afternoon or whatever. And I – I, I'd said to Gillian it's going to happen. And they were sort of doing all these unannounced visits and things and – I just let it – let it happen, and she was getting more and more upset. And you know [pause] I said well you, you can do it yourself and [pause] you know, but you – she – you just wouldn't do anything about it would you.
[pause] [he laughs a bit]

GILLIAN: [very quietly] No.

CAROLINE: So what happened, was the/

PATRICK: Oh y– well, I mean what happened was that um [pause] I mean I [pause] wrote them a letter in the end and said look er, you know, you can visit once a month [pause].

CAROLINE: Mm.

PATRICK: [pause] Um, you know, but that was it.
[In my separate interview with Gillian, eighteen months later, she had this to say:]

GILLIAN: I feel responsibility for [pause] relatives and er [longish pause] his and mine. Which he won't – accept. He knows I don't actually – like them and really want to see them because I *want* to see them. If I did, that would be – different, but I feel I ought to.

CAROLINE: Yes, yeah.

GILLIAN: And he doesn't think I ought to feel that. So he [pause] he says well [longish pause] he won't um, yes, act– he actually stops us I s'pose really.

CAROLINE: So how often do you see them?

GILLIAN: [pause] Well they come and see us, but we only go there, once a year.

CAROLINE: Right, right. And you feel a responsibility for that?

GILLIAN: Yes I do. And um.

CAROLINE: Do you think his parents look to you? You know, do you think they sort of put the responsibility on you in any way or?

GILLIAN: Oh [yes. Yes, they definitely do

CAROLINE: [They do?

GILLIAN: [pause] Mind you they can you know, that can make me feel the other way. His mother nags me, you know – When are you coming? When are you coming? and when – when she's said this the twentieth ti– [laughing] I say – we're not coming! – you know.

CAROLINE: Yeah. So when she phones up is she inclined to sort of speak to you then?

GILLIAN: Yes.

CAROLINE: Right.

GILLIAN: Oh yes, she speaks to me [said with feeling].

CAROLINE: Oh right – yes [both laughing] Hard luck! Yeah.

GILLIAN: But I also feel responsibility for my family and um [pause] yeah I have a brother who's mentally handicapped. And [longish pause] Patrick finds his vis– well we all do, his – his visits rather a trial, because I feel that er – it's my responsibility, he's my brother. Patrick says well, just because he's your brother doesn't mean [pause] we have to have him, you know.

CAROLINE: Mm [pause] And can – you don't see it like that?

GILLIAN: [longish pause] No not really. I think somebody has to have a responsibility.

There are four main points I want to make following the above extracts. First, Patrick seemed to have 'railroaded' the agenda in their relationship over whether responsibility for parents should be given priority. Perhaps he was in part able to do this because it was 'his parents' who were at issue here. However, by saying that such responsibility should not be prioritised, he was effectively failing to respect Gillian's value system, and denying the validity of her beliefs. Second, it is interesting to note from the above two extracts that Patrick's parents first called round to see Gillian, not Patrick, when they were staying close by on holiday. Furthermore, Gillian was clearly the person who was generally subjected to pressure from Patrick's mother concerning visits. I was told by both spouses that Patrick rarely spoke to his mother, but more than this, as I have pointed out above, responsibility for caring is generally seen by family members as, in the final analysis, the responsibility of women, not men. In this way, Gillian would probably be held 'responsible' for failure to fulfil family obligations. Third, and a related point here, is that by denying the validity of responsibility for caring – for her own family as well as his – Patrick is effectively undermining the work she puts in here and simultaneously providing a ready-made excuse for avoiding this onerous caring labour and leaving it all up to Gillian. Fourth, Gillian had been suffering from depression and clearly lacked confidence. Patrick's dialogue, above, seems unlikely to have the effect of making her feel better about herself.

In recent years feminist sociologists have begun to highlight the gendered and invisible nature of caring work, and to emphasise the fact that this caring work is hard labour (Mason 1996). I have already remarked that, during my interviews, almost without fail, it was the women who shouldered the burden of responsibility for the 'smoothness' of my visit. Other researchers (e.g. Cunningham-Burley 1984; McKee and O'Brien 1983) have pointed out that it is generally less socially acceptable for men to talk about family matters than it is for women and I have already suggested that on the whole women were more enthusiastic participants in my study than men. However, comments made by some of the women in my interviews suggested that it was quite a common pattern of behaviour for their husbands to, for example, get up and walk out of the room when they had company, behave unpredictably, sometimes rudely, or pick up a newspaper and leave the woman to do the entertaining. It would be hard to imagine any of these types of behaviour from a woman whose house you were visiting. All this underlines the point that, for women, 'responsibility for caring for others' generally extends to mean responsibility for social relations in general. Throughout the interviews, however, it was a common theme for wives' caring for others outside the family to go largely either unremarked or undermined by husbands and, as the above extract demonstrates, caring work overload could be constructed as the wife's fault for not 'putting her foot down' in the first place.

My disorganised wife

(I could do it better)

A second construction of a wife's inadequacy commonly present in men's accounts of division of labour involved the suggestion that stories of work overload from their wives must be related to a wife's incompetence rather than the demands of the work itself. For example, at various times during my interview with the Evanses, Rachael mentioned her dislike of housework and also that she finds child-care quite stressful. In the following extract from their joint interview, I would argue that Gordon's comments suggest that the 'problem' might lie with Rachael's organisational capacity:

RACHAEL: But I mean, how would you feel say if I were working full-time and you, you would be at home with the children? You wouldn't really like that – I don't know that I'd like that really I mean we – I don't know.

GORDON: I don't know. I, I'd probably um/

RACHAEL: I can't see you at toddler group – coping with that [I laugh].

GORDON: Well no it depen– it depends on the time – and what you can give to that particular thing. But, if, if you're at home, then <u>you've got to make your own life.</u>

RACHAEL: Yeah, but would you, could you do a kind of traditional, woman at home thing? I mean, would you want to do that?

GORDON: I'd be manic about housework. I mean I'd get it all – so spotlessly clean, I mean, you wouldn't be able to sit down without sort of, you know...I would, I know that because that's the way I am [she's laughing a bit]. Um [pause] I, I'd– I'd have to do it like that because <u>I'd have to keep that side of things – absolutely under control.</u>

RACHAEL: Well I used to try to be like that but you'd get very irritable if I'd say, don't sit there, or I've just done that or...

GORDON: Well no I, I – because then <u>I'd like to release myself to do more important, and more interesting things.</u>

RACHAEL: Mm.

In the above extract, Gordon's account contains a subtle implied criticism over the way Rachael handles her role as housekeeper and caregiver. In the first underlined sentence, we see him saying 'when you're at home you've got to make your own life', as if she doesn't. In the next underlined passage he says he would 'have to keep that side of things absolutely under control', also as if she doesn't. And here, Rachael clearly reads this as the implied meaning because she replies 'well I used to try to be like that but you'd get very irritable'. Gordon ignores this comment and ends by saying he'd release himself to do more important and interesting things. In other words, the whole job is rather unimportant anyway (he doesn't even mention child-care) and she is obviously 'making a meal of it'. The implication here, I would argue, is that, first, he could do it better than she could and, second, it is really Rachael's own fault if she is bogged down all day doing 'unimportant and uninteresting things'. It is also worth noting here that Rachael, as with Gillian in the earlier extract, has also been suffering from depression.

In another example of a husband implying bad management on the part of his wife, in Chapter 2, I discussed Karen and Will Craven's disagreements about how she ran the house. I used an example where Karen had implied that Will might be too critical but ended up saying it was her own fault. It is interesting here to draw on the comments Will made about this issue in his separate interview:

WILL: There's quite – there is a few things sometimes but I can't think what they are now. I – I've encouraged her, you know, and she might think I'm poking me nose in or something like – gotta – gotta get it over to her, the right way, or she thinks to herself 'oh flipping know-all – why can't he do it all' or somethin – bossing me about like [I'm laughing]. But um.

CAROLINE: What sort of things?

WILL: Well usually around the house – I come in an poke me nose in you see too often I s'pose. You know, if I can see that, you know, she's making hard work, or you know – could do it an easier way like, she says 'Oh well blooming know-all' [in funny voice] like. [laughing] But usually I'm only tryin to do it for her own good like. But um [pause] I dunno perhaps all women are the same. They don't like to be told like.

In other words, Will is effectively stating here, as with Gordon earlier, that he could do his wife's job better than she does. It is also interesting to note here that this kind of pattern was discovered by Mason (1987) in her study of older couples where husbands had retired and were therefore at home quite a lot and often seen by wives to be 'interfering' in their work as housekeeper. Mason points out that, for the wives in her sample, such 'interference' from husbands represented a threat to women's sense of control over this particular sphere of their lives, and I would argue that, for Karen, Will's behaviour in trying to 'tell her what to do' was likely to have been experienced in a similar threatening way.

It is also interesting to note here that Will's stance would have been likely to make it difficult for Karen to 'off-load' any of her tasks. Because she was likely to have experienced his 'interest' as a threat to her control of her domain, how could she then have safely asked him for assistance?

In saying that he is just trying to point things out 'for her own good', Will is adopting a patently patronising stance in relation to his wife. His account calls into question his wife's competence for a second time by suggesting that, not only isn't she doing things in a labour-saving way but, also, she does not have the good sense to learn from his advice. Not exactly bolstering of self-esteem. And again, as with the two previous examples of Gillian and Rachael above, Karen has been suffering from depression.

My 'brings it all on herself' wife

(She won't let me help)

The third construction of a wife's inadequacy I identified in my interview transcripts, also tied to the notion of female self-defeating behaviour, was connected to husbands' stories of wives' refusal to accept help from them and the implication that they bring the problem of subsequent work overload on themselves. Returning to the interviews with Heather and Gerry Morris, I discussed in Chapter 2 the way in which Heather suggested that conflict over keeping the house tidy must be her fault because she should be able to get more done. In Gerry's separate interview, I asked if anything Heather did ever reflected on him, and he had this to say:

GERRY: [long pause] Yeah, yeah. In one sense perhaps in that [pause] er, this is where we do have a little bit of a – a set to at times is, um, I don't like the house to be untidy if we've got people coming. That does bug me. Um, and I feel that, yeah in in that sense, her behaviour re– I feel reflects on me, yes, yes – yes. Er [pause] yeah we usually have a [pause] yeah if anybody's coming down for a weekend it's usually a mad scramble [laughing] to find somewhere to sit. Actually, we're pretty good tonight, but er, we've done most of it on Saturday.

It is interesting that in the above extract Gerry begins by implying that it is Heather's job to clean the house, i.e. her behaviour in not doing this reflects on him – and this ties in with Heather's version of events in her separate interview. However, by the end of the above extract Gerry is using 'we' to denote who did the tidying. In this connection, it is interesting to focus on the continuation of the above extract:

CAROLINE: Yeah right. Do you have fairly clear lines of who does what and things like that?

GERRY: Um [pause] Yeah. I th– I think that's one side where I fall down probably cause um [pause] Heather does tend to, p'rhaps carry more than her fair share of of, sort of, domestic duties if you like. But I still maintain she's her own worst enemy because if you do go out to try and assist – she's interfering [I laugh a bit], she won't let you get on and – and help you know, um, amazingly, but er, [pause] yeah well um [pause] yeah, I might go out there to sort of, you know, if we've got say someone coming I'll say, well look, I'll do the washing up you – you, you can go and do this or go up the shops or do whatever else you want to do. I can do this, and tidy up the kitchen. And then you sort of – two minutes later and she – she's sort of, scrabbling round – sort of putting something away and, and I think oh, well this is a total waste of time me helping, because I'm not saving her any time because she's not doing anything – you know – we do er…[pause]

From the phrasing of the first sentence Gerry now seems quite keen to reconstruct fairness, whereas in his previous extract he may have created a rather 'unegalitarian' position in front of me – i.e that he expects her to tidy up the house for him and his friends. He therefore commences by suggesting that he may in some ways not be doing enough in the house. However, by the third line he switches this problematising of himself and puts in a 'but'. Following the 'but', we have an account of how essentially it is Heather's fault that Gerry doesn't help her in the house. She is, he argues, 'her own worst enemy'. Furthermore, in the last underlined phrase, he talks about her 'scrabbling round' in the kitchen – not a particularly positive image of his wife.

Mansfield and Collard (1988) and also Mason (1987) identify similar patterns in their data from their studies of younger and older married couples respectively. Although Mansfield and Collard do not interrogate this phenomenon, Mason argues, linking to the point made earlier, that older women refusing 'help' from their retired husbands can be understood in terms of an attempt to hold on to the one sphere within which she has historically had a form of 'circumscribed' control. Mason also makes the point that husbands' 'help' was often seen by women as more of a hindrance, and this was something that was commented on by some of the women in my sample. In fact, Heather Morris alludes to this point when she tells me herself that Gerry says she's 'her own worst enemy'. She tells me that she likes things put back into their proper place. In the same way, Cathy Thompson had this to say in her separate interview:

CATHY: It's alright when he's going to work but, like I said before, when he's got a couple of weeks off then I'll get irritated then because I can't see why – I should carry on, working, as it were, and him not. And that does irritate me. Cause I think he should do more when he's at home.

CAROLINE: So what does he say? Do you row about that? – do you point that out or?

CATHY: [pause] Yes – I mean, he'll do something like – he'll say ah I'll cook the tea. So he'll cook the tea, and then the kitchen's just [pause]/

CAROLINE: [Like a bomb's hit it.

CATHY: [A wreck [both laughing a bit]. And I think, well so what. He's cooked the tea but now I gotta [pause] do all this.

It is interesting to note in the above extract that Cathy and my simultaneous comments indicate my own familiarity with this particular 'phenomenon'. Constructing a version of events where the 'problem' is construed as the wife's reluctance to let the husband help, functions first to absolve the husband from responsibility for housekeeping and child-care, and second, implicitly suggests that the problem lies in the wife's 'self-defeating' and irrational behaviour. There is little room in this version of events for an acknowledgement of skill or expertise on the part of a wife. Cathy and I, together, in the above extract are trying to construct an alternative view where Cathy's behaviour starts to look more rational.

My lucky wife
(*The easy life*)

When I asked Marion Hughes – who had sole responsibility for child-care and housework and whose husband had been unemployed for six years – if she thought it was harder for women than men in marriage, she said:

MARION: Um [pause] Yeah. I think it is. I mean, probably some men wouldn't agree with it but [pause] I do because they [women], seem to be [pause] left doing everything, if you see what I mean sort of. I mean, if they've got a job, they can't come home and sit down and relax. They've gotta come in and perhaps start on the tea or the – or the supper or whatever, you know, or sort of doing the housework and that. So I mean, it's not – it's more difficult for a woman than it is a man. I mean when – when the man goes out to work, comes home and sits down and [pause] perhaps that's it I mean, he may potter out in the garden – for a couple of hours – depending on what the weather's like you know.

As far as most of the men in my study group were concerned, it seemed Marion was right; they would *not* have been likely to agree with her. The notion that their wives had an easy life – or that they were actually very lucky – was common in my interviews. I have already discussed ways in which the women would tend to overlook their own paid work when accounting for their division of labour as fair. This pattern was also true for the men in my sample. Women's paid employment often appeared to be perceived by quite a few of the men as either a 'hobby' for the women, or an irritating necessity for supplementing income, rather than real sacrifice for the family – as was the man's work. In this respect, for example, Mike Walters, in his separate interview, illustrated this point when he told me how he had to cook the Sunday dinner nowadays because Liz worked at the weekends:

MIKE: I think we er [pause] manage alright there, with the, the role change at the weekend. It's er, it's 10 o'clock she's at work, and I'm at home so – I have to do things like – cook the Sunday dinner, which she gets out of doing you know…

Mike called the weekend arrangements 'role change' although Liz in her separate interview told me that weekend working simply meant she needed to get everything prepared in advance. However, it is interesting to note that whichever 'role' Mike was playing at whichever time, he implied that he had drawn the 'short straw'. For example, above he states that Liz 'gets out of doing' the Sunday dinner when she goes to work implying that his role here is the most onerous. However, in their joint interview, Mike had this to say about the role of housewife:

MIKE: They say housewives work hard at home but um – they do find a fair bit of leisure [pause] whether they're sat down with the children or not is – they're still sat down and – television gets watched quite a bit.

Although Mike is talking about 'housewives generally' in this extract (as with the hypothetical accounts in the previous chapter), his wife's response to his utterance (which I will look at shortly) demonstrates that she thinks he is talking about her. For now though, I would make the point that Mike's notion that household chores and child-care are easier than breadwinning (except when he was doing them) appeared to be an implicit (and sometimes explicit) view of most of the men I interviewed. For example, the following extract is taken from a difficult interview with Wendy and Neil Spencer. Neil Spencer was one of the few men in my study whose behaviour bordered on rude. He took no responsibility for the interview at all, was often monosyllabic and left before the end. Throughout, he made no pretence of 'helping' at all with any of the domestic, child-care (or indeed home maintenance) chores:

NEIL: Well a normal day for me is, I get up at quarter past 6. I start work at quarter past 7 so I leave here at about 7 o'clock – by which time Wendy and the kids are just stirring [pause] and um, she gets up, gets them fed and watered and clothed and, ready for school and chucks them out and –
WENDY: And has got nothing to do all day [sarcastically].
[pause]
NEIL: Then she sits down, a lady of leisure all day [she and I laugh a bit]. Now she'll tell you what she does.

Although to some extent Neil presented this remark as 'not really meant' – by saying, 'now she'll tell you what she does', Wendy's retort to his first comment implied that this construction of events was familiar to her and they had had this discussion before. I think these types of remarks by the men were actually 'toned down' or perhaps suppressed, in the main because of the way in which I was perceived and herein lay the 'threat' for men in Neil's position. He was at some level publicly accountable to present their relationship as based on principles of equality and yet he needed to fend off Wendy's challenge. In the end, he left the interview early and went out.

In the same way, Malcolm Anderson occasionally implied a similar idea about the easiness of his wife's job in the joint interviews. For example, in this extract where I had asked them to describe each other to me, Sarah described Malcolm as hard working, but his description of her, couched rather as an apology, hinted that he may be less sure about her:

SARAH: I dunno, I think Malcolm's kind, generous, very hard working [pause] don't complain very much – basically a very nice person [laughing].

MALCOLM: Oh dear.

SARAH: I can – I can't be more honest than that I don't think, no. He hasn't got any really bad points, not really.

MALCOLM: Mm. Um, that's what I think about Sarah really, I mean, you sort of have a joke about er...

SARAH: Money? [laughing]

MALCOLM: housework she does, you know, I sort of take the mick at times but it is – meant – as a joke, you know, I realise she works hard with the kids and one thing and another...

And then in the second interview, when talking about potential role reversal, he says:

MALCOLM: Maybe I'm a bit old fashioned in that respect like you know. Um, a lot of young couples would probably go for um you know a bloke might say I'd love – time home, with the kids, and – have an easier life – or they'd consider it an easier life until they try it, you kn– obviously you know [laughing a bit]. Er – I wouldn't like it meself, no.

In both of these extracts there is a suggestion from Malcolm that Sarah's role is less arduous than his – albeit he 'corrects himself' on each occasion.

The point about constructing housework and childcare as easy is that (1) problems women might be experiencing are positioned as even more obviously their own fault and (2) the traditional homemaker/breadwinner division of labour can be construed by implication as fair on the woman and even possibly unfair on the man.

Drawing together the four themes I have identified so far, all were common in men's accounts of division of labour within their relationship and all involved implicitly blaming women for any perceived inequalities. She's put upon, she's disorganised, she won't let me help and, when it comes down to it, it's a really easy job. In all these constructions the husband, by implication, seemed to be suggesting that he could do the job better than the wife. But herein lies the rub, because when it came to it, all the men pointed out that they actually wouldn't be able to do the job at all.

The biologically driven wife

(*My wife with the extra little something*)

Although comments from men often implied that they thought their wives had an easy life, when pushed, all the men said that a role reversal would be inappropriate in their case because their wives were much better suited to look after the children given that they had what seemed to amount to an 'extra little something'. This pattern bears a striking similarity to the pattern identified by Philips and Taylor (1980) (and also see Coyle 1984). Philips and Taylor discuss the ways in which skill divisions in the clothing industry were developed through the struggle of unionised men to retain craft dominance. As part of the construction of the continued gender divisions of labour in this industry, women's work, these authors argued, was simultaneously complimented and devalued through the concept of 'nimble fingers'. Returning to my own data, with the Scotts, for example (a couple who did not have children at the time) Tom Scott told me that role reversal would be inappropriate for them because he did not have much patience. Emma, he pointed out, had much more patience with their cat than he did. In similar fashion, Gerry Morris had this to say when I asked him about role reversal:

GERRY: I think – I think personally, I – I – I th– a role reversal wouldn't have worked. It it would work, maybe now – but when the children were very small I don't think it would have worked very well at all – I think Heather's um – Heather's patience is um – infinitely greater than mine [laughing]. [pause] No I think that would have been – um [pause] difficult for us.

In a similar, but slightly more effusive way, Gordon Evans has the following to say about why his wife is particularly good at care-giving:

GORDON: Um, I think [pause] it's a shame really that I mean I enjoy my job, but at the end of the day sometimes I'm, I'm wrung out, you know. I, I've got very little left, to give. And in a way I resent the fact that if I come home and I'm absolutely sort of knackered that Peter will jump all over me and Jason will say did you see this, they and this, and my response won't be as lively as I would like. Because I'm worn out. Um [pause] Rachael on the other hand I think is is, she she's terrific. She's much much more creative, much more patient, um, and much more gifted, with, with the children, she really is. I mean she, I've got nothing but admiration for the way she [pause] she conscientiously puts in the, the, she – there's lots of input. And er, I think the children, are – they are – they will never really know, just how well blessed they are with her as a mother. She really is superb.

Brian Thompson, in the following example, refers rather to some elusive 'tuning in' mechanism, and suggests this might be physical:

BRIAN: Um [pause] the only reason women are better is because they've been sort of – trained I think, through the, through the years. I think men could do it just as well through the– apart from the obvious, practical things you know. Um – yeah, I don't think there's any reason why women are b– but they do, to be honest, certainly with the kids, um, they do seem to be, tuned into them a little bit better. Must be some sort of physical thing. Um, because when they cry at night men, m– mo– a lot of men don't seem to hear it where the women do.

In Brian's account, the 'biological' underpinning of his construction of women's ability can be seen quite clearly, and this construction of the extra little something as natural was a consistent theme. And, again, the strong biological underpinnings of the notion of the extra little something come through in the following extract from Jim Wright:

JIM: Um [long pause] If men didn't have to go to work, I think men could probably do it as well [caregiving]. Um – there's certain touches [pause] that women have [pause] um – Amanda's actually excellent at, sort of explaining things to, to Henry and you know, he's sort of 'why is this, why is that?' which – I wouldn't – be so good at. I'm [pause] and, you know, she seems to be in certain aspects better sort of, er, but I mean if it wasn't for work I mean if I was here all day and it was my job to look after them if she was out at work, the roles were totally reversed like that, I think I could cope just as well, but there'd be certain, there'd be certain aspects [pause] that wouldn't be a woman's [pause] that only a woman could give.

CAROLINE: Yeah, yeah.

JIM: Sort of thing there's certain – probably that little extra tenderness sort of thing, um [pause] you know/

CAROLINE: Do you think a role reversal would in some cases be a good thing, or a bad thing or?

JIM: [pause] Well for – for us?

CAROLINE: Not necessarily for you.

JIM: Oh for any – Er [pause] well I s'pose in certain [pause] again it depends on the man – no I don't think so myself, generally I should think, cause I think that little extra touch that a woman can give [pause] is essential to, to the family. Er, and if she's – her head's all tied up with business or what have you – work – she wouldn't be able to give that sort of touch at the end of the day sort of thing cause she'd probably come back absolutely shattered sort of thing and [pause] in much the same way as that a man might come back, you know, and not listening so much and not, feel, quite so caring and I think the, woman does have that touch sort of thing. But I – I see no reason why a man can't physically go through the – and bring up the family.

Sometimes, women in my study referred to their husbands' lack of patience as a way of defending their own skill, as in the following account (already partially reproduced in the 'Easy life' section) with Liz and Mike Walters:

MIKE: They say housewives work hard at home but um – they do find a fair bit of leisure time [pause] whether they're sat down with the children or not is – they're still sat down and – television gets watched quite a bit.

LIZ: Yeah children necessarily aren't physically er – tiring. They're mentally exhausting [slight awkward laugh].

CAROLINE: Yeah – mm. And/

LIZ: I mean you sometimes have trouble just for a few hours [slight laugh from me] [pause] or half an hour.

MIKE: I'm a touch more short-tempered perhaps yeah. Less tolerant.

LIZ: I mean if you ask Bobbie what Daddy hasn't got, he'll tell you he hasn't got any patience [I laugh] And that's at two and a half!

I think the construction of the extra little something functioned to protect men from direct challenge to the existing child-care arrangements because, as the above account illustrates, through this construction women were unable to obtain suitable support and acknowledgement from their husbands of the very real difficulties they faced in coping with the job. Although Mike acknowledges above that he might be a 'touch more short-tempered' than his wife, such an acknowledgement is of no real help to Liz if tolerance is seen as an inherently female quality. By this analysis, he has not got it because he's a man (and therefore *ought* not really to have it). She *has* got it because she's a woman and therefore this should make the job easy for her. If she copes with the job she is no more than being true to her biology. The construction of the 'extra little something' effectively robbed women of a way legitimately to complain about the difficulties of their job.

It is interesting that if coping, in a biological argument, is no more than being true to female biology, not coping can also be biologised in a similar way. To explain what I mean here I want to return for a moment to interview data from Sarah and Malcolm Anderson. Although Sarah was one of the few women in my study who early on in the interview made a fairly formal statement about the traditional but fair nature of their division of labour (see p. 16) throughout both interviews with this couple Sarah nevertheless was clearly unhappy with various aspects of her life. I have reproduced an extract on page 71 where Malcolm suggests that the housewife/caregiver role is easy. However, quite often in response to Sarah's challenges he kept fairly quiet, and occasionally came up with placating comments, as for example when Sarah states, when talking about caring for children:

SARAH: Yeah [it's a] bit frustrating sometimes, in't it, if you got them all day cause I mean I'm with Susan from [half past 7 in the morning till
MALCOLM: [Well it's a lot on you yeah.

However, Malcolm made no suggestion here of thinking of ways to alleviate the pressure on Sarah. In the following account, both Sarah and Malcolm effectively 'medicalise' the problems that Sarah is experiencing. This is a joint account and in fact Sarah instigates the discussion of her 'problem'. However, there is a germ of a different perspective in Sarah's comments although she is unable to get this perspective directly onto the marital agenda:

SARAH: I blow up a bit, yeah. Yeah I do sometimes. I, I s'pose it's PMT you put it down to really, you know. The week before my period's due I'm – pretty awful to live with. But I can't help it [all laughing]. I s'pose I do get a bit short tempered and a bit irritable and [pause] things which p'rhaps you wouldn't take a lot of notice of the rest of the time, sort of really get to you a bit, you know. Um/
CAROLINE: Can you give me a for instance, of the sort of thing that – you know?
SARAH: [pause]
CAROLINE: Or could you think of something last week or something?
SARAH: Well p'rhaps with the oldest girl, maybe I [pause] really sort of blow up at her whereas maybe I'd sort of [pause] be a bit more rational and think well, she's growing up. A lot of it's her age and hormones and all this sort of thing you know. But, you know, you can't handle it sort of quite so well and/
CAROLINE: And then how would that, you know, say like if you [Malcolm] come home then, do you sort of talk about that, or would you – what would you – how would you find out?
MALCOLM: Um.
SARAH: I've got a bottle of vitamin B6 in the cupboard, he puts it out for me very discreetly [so he [laughing].
MALCOLM: [Yeah, yeah. Not so discreetly Sarah, I just slam it on the [nearest
SARAH: [You put it where I can see it yeah! so [both laughing]. But I think he understands and realises why I'm like it. There's nothing – personal
MALCOLM: Yeah, [it's frustrating and annoying at the time, and I know that…
SARAH: [to do with Malcolm you know.
MALCOLM: Sarah knows she's like it, and can't do anything about it but [pause]
SARAH: It's like you're a different person [for that week, I should say, you know.
MALCOLM: [Yeah, yeah. Um.

SARAH: Don't like yourself very much. I don't know what other people think about you [laughing a bit – put as a bit of a question] but – on the other hand I always feel better when I'm out of the house, you know. The pressure seems to be a bit relieved then.

[he and me 'mm']

SARAH: I think oh…housework! I always think of moving, when I'm like that as well [me laughing].

MALCOLM: Oh yeah, I was just gonna say that yeah, yeah.

SARAH: Oh this big house! lets get a – nice modern little box and not much housework. Everything sort of gets on top of you, then it passes and I'm alright again then.

Here, Sarah commences by couching her problems in biological terms although (in the kind of debating style referred to in Chapter 2) she attempts an alternative explanation at the end of the extract when she says she feels better if she gets out of the house and it is housework that gets her down. However, the prevailing mode of explanation in this extract is a biological one with Sarah finally saying that the problem 'passes and I'm alright again' – rather like the passing of an illness.

Malcolm actively helps Sarah to construct this biological explanation here and, once again, we see the overall effect of woman-blame – albeit here the blame is located in Sarah's biology. Paradoxically, in constructing such an account, Malcolm was helping to create a version of reality that suggested that it was Sarah's biology (i.e. PMT) that prevented her behaving in a biologically 'natural' (i.e. patient) way. Yet, throughout the whole of their joint interviews Sarah appears to be trying in various places to 'cry out' about the difficulties she is experiencing in terms of her role. And with a teenage daughter, a second daughter approaching her teens and a toddler (who was a 'surprise' to the couple) to look after, plus the work Sarah does at play-group, and the fact that both spouses admit that Sarah has to run the home single-handedly, how surprising is Sarah's depression? Yet at various places in the interview Malcolm suggests that Sarah possesses the 'extra little something' that makes her ideally suited to domestic work.

As a final point here, although a common theme in the interviews was for men to explain the impossibility of a role change for them in terms of their admiration for a proposed 'extra little something' that their wives possessed, there were other places in interviews where a rather different version of reality emerged. For example, Gordon (see p. 72) had talked effusively about his wife's creativity with the children when asked whether role change would be possible for him. However, when asked by his wife earlier how he would cope if there was a role change between them he talked about needing to be organised in order to release himself to do 'more important and more interesting things'. And again, returning to the interviews with the Andersons, not only has Malcolm in the above extract helped Sarah to biologise her account of her experiences, towards the end of the joint interview, the following conversation ensues between the couple:

MALCOLM: I couldn't do your job all day long really. I don't think so – you know.
SARAH: Well it's too boring isn't it? [pause] I mean if you've been used to using your [brain I mean [pause]
MALCOLM: [Well.
SARAH: I feel like I'm a cabbage sometimes [laughing a little bit].
MALCOLM: Mm. [pause] I can't imag– I can't imagine meself in that situation, not really, you know.

By constructing the care-giving role as based in female biology, Malcolm is protecting himself from taking on aspects of the role. Furthermore, by constructing 'the problem' of Sarah's depression in the earlier extract as biological, Malcolm was effectively denying her access to the very type of explanation she offers above for why he would not be able to do her job – namely, that it might be a problematic job. Finally, by concurring with her assessment of her role as boring and not about using her brain, he is effectively implying that he sees her role as inferior.

In sum, I would argue that the utility of the construction of the extra little something for men was that, whilst allowing them to give the impression that they could 'technically' do the job quite easily if necessary, such a construction also implied that men could not really do the job because it was women's work.

The construction of the more than adequate husband

In the first section of this chapter I examined ways in which men construct negative images of their wives. In this section I outline ways in which I believe men, on the other hand, tended to construct a positive picture of self.

Your clever husband

The first conversational practice that was present in interviews with husbands involved sustained celebration of their own skills and achievements – often at apparently rather inappropriate moments. Some of the men would happily talk for long periods about their paid employment or home maintenance skills, whereas there often seemed to be a tacit agreement between the couples that the woman's work – either paid employment or domestic labour – was too boring to discuss. The following extract from the joint interview with Carol and Tony Matthews was a good example of this. Tony was unemployed when I interviewed the couple (and it is interesting to note here that both spouses talked about their family support benefit as 'his money'). Carol had major responsibility for housework and child-care and also helped out at the local play-group although she was not in paid employment outside the home. Tony had a strong tendency to turn even the most apparently unrelated topic into a monologue about his skill at home maintenance. For example, in the following extract from their joint interview, I had just asked them what made them decide to get married:

TONY: Um, We just sort of felt it was right.

CAROL: Um, I can't think of anything else – just mutual [laughing]

TONY: Well, within a – well as I say we started going out on November 9th [pause] and before the Christmas of that year um, I'd already [pause] down her mother's house there's the archway, where we got the archway there [pointing] – there was a cupboard, built in there. It had been closed and panelled over, and papered over for thirteen years. And before the Christmas I'd already had that opened.

CAROL: It was within a fortnight.

TONY: Within a fortnight was it? I know it was pretty quick. I stripped all that lot out, and I built her a nice archway in there – put a light in there and whatever, and built a unit in down the bottom. I think it was just after Christmas I did the rest of it, all the way along wan't it. Sort of, fairly similarish to this [pointing] I mean instead of having the top up there we had the top down there for the tele didn't we. So I stripped all the grate out and everything, didn't I. Rebuilt a new wood fire [laughing].

CAROLINE: They were quite pleased about you getting married then?

[My last question is an attempt to put the conversation back on track!]

With one or two of the couples in particular, such monologues from husbands about their own work seemed particularly hurtful given that wives in my study clearly had a problem with their own identities as 'part-time' workers and mothers. Men emphasising the importance of their own contribution was likely to have the effect of 'rubbing salt in the wounds' for a wife who, not only had problems with her own role, but had experienced her husband undermining this role in the same interview by saying that he could do it better, or that it was easy really, or that she was marvellous at it 'because she was a woman' but he would not be able to do such a [boring] job himself. In the above extract, it is likely that Tony felt the need to celebrate his home maintenance skills in this way, partly because he was unemployed. However, in-depth discussions from men about their abilities and skills, whether at home maintenance or in paid employment, were common. On the other hand, lengthy discussions with women about their own perceived skills and expertise simply did not occur.

Your 'better than most' husband

The second conversational practice I identified in my data that functioned to construct the man's contribution as better than adequate involved using a comparative device. In the same way that women sometimes used a comparative device to reconstruct an account of fairness in their relationship – i.e. 'he's much better than other husbands' – so too did men quite often take this line in both joint and separate discussions. For example, Jim Wright had this to say at one point in his separate interview:

JIM: No, what does annoy me is when, somebody does sort of make an off – sort of off the cuff remark sort of thing like um – oh um [pause] you know – 'all men' you know, 'bla bla bla' you know, something a bit silly. I think, when was the last time you bloody cooked the meals when – as soon as you come back in from doing a [pause] so/

CAROLINE: Can you give me a for instance then? What what…

JIM: Oh [pause] my sister actually said – made some [pause] er it wasn't really directed at me she said 'Oh well, Men!' sort of thing, you know, and it really bugged me that. I thought I, I haven't – I, I sweat my heart out and sort of – doing this sort of thing and that. So I er yeah I mean I did fly off the handle a bit at her. I said, you know, when did your bloody husband like, get the bloody ironing board out like you know, I mean, lazy git he is [laughing].

Or, in extracts already quoted earlier from Richard Price and Gordon Evans:

RICHARD: Well I can only speak for our, for for us. I mean I – [pause] although my Dad does the housework as well. But I'm sure [pause] his era was – the women do the housework, the men go out to work. Well I s'pose a lot of blokes still – feel that way. In fact a lot of my friends obviously do. But um [pause] personally I – the house is as much my responsibility as Margaret's and in fact it's usually me that does – you know – we split it 50–50.

And then again, with Gordon Evans:

GORDON: I think in middle-class um, families, and I s'pose we, because of our jobs and so on, and our attitudes, would be considered middle class, I don't know. But certainly people like us, expect a much more balanced partnership between husband and wife. I think in working class families, from what I know, um, there's still fairly sort of – prejudiced, chauvinist attitudes by men. Er, you know – 'I wouldn't do that. That's women's work' you know. That means they'd never change a nappy on their own children. They never cook any food. So on and so forth. I think it's er – middle-class and educated people realise that that's hardly the way to to make a balanced relationship.

And then again with Peter Docherty:

PETER: Well my – I think compared to a lot of the couples we know, I think I'm pretty good in terms of actually, you know [pause] doing other things around the house. Washing up [pause] ironing I'll do sometimes if [pause], as I say we tend to do the same things you know, I'll happily do it. I'm much more considerate I think than many of my [pause] male [pause] um friends. Certainly one of them I know he's a lazy git!

And then again with Patrick Henderson:

PATRICK: I – I think I do more housework than most husbands do. And I think I'm more sort of child orientated than most – most men are.

And so on.

If men conceded that they might not do as much as they could, or be as perfect as they might be, explanations were generally couched in terms of the 'self-defeating' housewife, i.e. 'I'd like to help but she won't let me'. In fact, at this stage it is worth reflecting back to the point raised earlier in the book when I indicated that inequalities in society were overwhelmingly described as relating to the sphere of work, and if related to marriage, never directly to one's own marriage. I would add here that although most of the men in my study group conceded at some level that things may be less than fair for women in the workplace, only one man, Bernard Hardy, suggested that existing patterns of inequality might be in any way the fault of men. The predominant reasons given for inequality can be seen reflected in the following extract from the separate interview with Patrick Henderson:

CAROLINE: Why do you think there are these, you know – that women perhaps don't have an equal deal with pay and things like that? Why do you think there are these inequalities?

PATRICK: Well I used to think that it was because, you know, it was <u>all the mother's fault</u> [laughing] – that they have influence over the children – <u>the way they bring them up.</u>

CAROLINE: Right.

PATRICK: But um [pause] I have seen, <u>differences</u> which um, you know are – are – due to sex in young children, which do <u>seem to be innate</u> – based on my personal experience. I don't like to admit that, I think they should be um, you know, free to do whatever they want but er [pause] you know.

Namely, (1) it's women's fault (2) it's conditioning (3) it's the fault of women's biology. What is more, eight out of the seventeen men interviewed made comments to the effect that perhaps 'things might be going too far the other way now' – in other words, far from women being oppressed in this society, things were now becoming, or about to become, 'ever so slightly unfair' on men.

Drawing the conversational practice together, the potential net effect of such discourses was to construct a version of reality where the husband was depicted as *more than* adequate against a backdrop where wives were depicted as *less than* adequate. From within such a construction, men were well placed to construct a version of reality in which they were 'slightly hard done by' in relation to their wives. This brings me to the final conversation practice I want to identify here.

Your overloaded husband

(My underloaded wife)

The final conversational practice I want to discuss in this section involved another comparative process, this time depicting the husband's contribution to the relationship as excessive in relation to the wife. Male sacrifice for the family is a phenomenon on which other researchers have commented. For example, Hunt (1980) argued two decades ago that women's work tends to be rendered invisible by being treated as an expression of love, whereas men's work outside the home is highly visible. In the following example of such a construction from a joint interview with Gerry Morris, we see the familiar construction of the housewife's role as 'easy', whilst at the same time Gerry depicts his own contribution as almost intolerably stressful:

GERRY: I think um [long pause] I think sometimes [pause] the responsibi– you know I feel an awful responsibility to the family and – to Heather and to, you know, keeping the house and, whatever else, and, I sup– I suppose just very occasionally there's a little bit of resentment creeps in. Um [pause] I don't – it's not that I resent that you're not working or anything like that, but um – perhaps it's envy. I envy Heather's lifestyle a great deal. You know, she seems as though she's a free agent. [pause] Which is probably not true [laughing], cause she's two kids hanging around but it, it gives the impression that…

HEATHER: Yeah

Another example of this comparative process can be seen in the following dialogue with Emma and Tom Scott:

TOM: [talking about his job] It's just a good day if I have a lunch break but, it's normally sort of hectic and it's, you know, constant graft, all day really.

EMMA: He occasionally, so he says, grabs a pasty from the cold cabinet and scoffs it while filling in forms or whatever it is.

TOM: Um, that's right. Administration. So that, that's basically the day then. Normal Friday that is [all laughing]. I do finish a bit early on a Friday sometimes, about half past five. By which time you've got a bit more time to spend with each other then, to do little things or whatever.

CAROLINE: Right. So, but on a weekday again, what time do you finish?

TOM: Weekday, Monday Tuesday Wednesday it's normally 8 till 5.30. But Thursday and Fridays until 8 till 8.

CAROLINE: Extraordinarily long hours isn't it?

TOM: Oh, excessive.

CAROLINE: Oh dear me.

TOM: Soul destroying I can tell you. It really is. [pause] Especially when I see, you know, Emma, with all this [pause] leisure time.

EMMA: Yes [as in, 'yes but'].

TOM: But it's not really because theoretically you're supposed to er…[I cut in at this point and start to talk about the stress of doing Emma's type of job.]

In the above example, Tom invokes a picture of the 'lucky housewife' by suggesting that Emma has 'all this leisure time' although Emma is engaged in full-time employment. Counterposed to this he constructs a vision of his own workload as almost intolerable, and it is interesting to note, above, that I help Tom construct this picture (albeit I consciously cut in at the end of the extract to try to support Emma). suggesting that the notion of male sacrifice is as well entrenched in our making sense processes as is the notion of woman-blame.

These accounts of male sacrifice counterposed with 'the easy life' for women had the potential to 'guilt trip' wives, I think, as the following extended dialogue from Heather and Gerry demonstrates. When I interviewed the Morrises, Gerry had been suffering with bouts of depression since the birth of their first child. These extracts are taken from the first and second joint interviews with the couple:

[on getting married:]

GERRY: I, I – I can remember feeling, cause we, at the same time we had an extension built on the house and, sort of taking on more financial commitments. More finance and a wife! God, I hope I'm doing the right thing.

[on the birth of their first child:]

GERRY: Well, I s'pose it screwed me up basically – didn't it?

HEATHER: It did, yes. You were really quite ill.

CAROLINE: Were you really. W/

GERRY: Yeah [something inaudible].

HEATHER: He got the depression not me.

GERRY: Yeah.

HEATHER: You know, post-natal depression.

CAROLINE: Right.

HEATHER: I – I was alright but we, we had/

GERRY: It wasn't exactly post-natal depression was it? [a bit scathingly]

HEATHER: No, but, you know. Um [pause] as soon as, we knew I was pregnant, we stopped using my money, and we lived off Gerry's just to, you know, make sure that we could do that. And we managed that no trouble didn't we?

GERRY: Mm.

HEATHER: And so you know, we'd had, we had quite a bit saved really by the time [pause] she was actually here, and of course I got – maternity pay as well, for a while. But um [pause] it still knocked you for six didn't it really?

GERRY: Mm.

HEATHER: I think it was just you know the g– millstone. All these responsibilities. And it wasn't really that long – after we were married, was it. Well, you know.

[and on the second child:]

HEATHER: Well you, it got so bad [child crying in the night] that he had to move in with – with Mary [elder child] to sleep. He was in the bottom bunk, weren't you?

GERRY: [pause] Yeah/

HEATHER: Because, he was just no good for work.

GERRY: But you see I took on, I took a lot, I took yeah, but I think I was taking a lot of precautions. Um, I always think I was probably defending myself to some extent, in that, um, I didn't attend the birth – I was there, in the waiting room – but I wouldn't go in – to the birth.

HEATHER: No, no. I wish it had been the other way round now. That he'd seen Barry born and not Mary.

GERRY: Well wh/

CAROLINE: Why?

HEATHER: Because it was so easy, so quick.

CAROLINE: Yeah, yeah.

HEATHER: Incredibly quick.

GERRY: [sounding cross] Perhaps you don't then understand why I stayed away/

HEATHER: No – no but, from a – from what I went through with you being with me – do you see what I mean?

GERRY: Yeah, yeah. Perhaps I do.

HEATHER: Yeah – [I know.

GERRY: [But I'm not sure that that really [slight awkward laugh] was why I stayed away!

HEATHER: No, no – naturally.

GERRY: I was, I was trying to distance myself a little bit from the second one because I was concerned about having the same sort of problems as we'd had with the first one.

[and then, almost at the end of the second joint interview:]

GERRY: But, I think that...if Heather, you know, if you went back sort of six years, and and we didn't have the family, and Heather was still working, I would, probably find it – I don't want to make you feel guilty – but I think I would probably find it easier, to perhaps have a crack at something new, um, than I do at the moment, because I do [pause] feel, a great responsibility to [pause] you [know, to feed

HEATHER: [Yes.

GERRY: and clothe the children if you like. It sounds corny I know, but er...

Not surprisingly, given the above, the whole of Heather's separate interview is peppered with fears about holding Gerry back, and with constructions of self-blame.

The above dialogue between Gerry and Heather Morris can, I think, be seen as an extreme example of 'guilt tripping' but I also want to underline the point here that hardly any of the men held back from telling me and their wives how difficult things were for them and how their experienced problems might be their wife's fault. So, for example, in the following extract from Will Craven, where he has been talking about the difficulties he experiences with his life as a farmer:

WILL: And I've always, you know, it was only, I could never ever start any farm of my own, you know, not these days. I, you know, I just haven't got the capital like. Then, you know, it [her family farm] was the nearest thing that I was ever gonna get to a farm, you know, to a house and a farm/

KAREN: You make it sound as though you married me to get down here! [laughing]

However, whether or not Will felt himself fortunate in having acquired the farm through marriage, in other places in the interview he gave the opposite impression. Karen in her separate interview suggests that she worries Will might want to leave the farm, and in the same way, in his separate interview with me, he had this to say on the subject of disagreements:

WILL: Um [pause] usually when I – I said oh, well let's go somewhere. She said well how can we we aint got any money. An that spar– that gets me goin then. I said well if we hadn't of 'mming' come ere in the first place I said, we'd have – I've stayed where I was too, I said we'd ave plenty of money. But um, all stems back to Karen. She always wanted to move ere see. She always wanted to come here. She had her heart set on it. An – cause I had a good job where I – on tother side of the village like – had a good, very good job there, in farming, and I had good prospects as well like, but I give it up, to come here, and that usually pops – I usually say well I give up a good job to come here. I say, look what I got landed – landed us into, you know.

Whatever the rights and wrongs of a situation that involves complicated and gendered kinship customs and practices, the point I want to make here is that Will constructed an account of the situation in this interview that explicitly and unequivocally located the blame for this particular state of affairs with Karen and there was considerable evidence in both interviews with Karen that this was a familiar construction and that Karen felt guilty. Yet Karen never engaged in such an unequivocal practice in reverse and nor did any of the other women in my study.

Although women also took the opportunity of the interview to put across their point of view – and I have already given examples in Chapter 3 – concerted attempts to blame the man rarely occurred within the women's dialogue. (Nor did they function in the same undermining way – a point I will take up in Chapter 5.) Rather, comments that appeared as criticisms were generally hastily counterbalanced with a positive or conciliatory comment to offset this negative effect. For example, Joan Docherty – in her joint interview – sometimes appeared openly to challenge her husband for not doing anything with the children. However, she generally stopped short of 'going too far' – particularly when Peter showed any sign of remorse for his behaviour. It is interesting to note here that, in her separate interview, she also told me that the family may have 'held Peter back', a point that Peter himself referred to in his own separate interview.

Summary

I have attempted to show in this chapter that, working from a structurally and economically uneven playing field in which they were at a considerable social advantage:

1 Men were engaging in a number of conversational practices within the interview context that could serve to deflect wives' challenges to the status quo of the relationship without explicitly laying bare the gendered inequalities that permeated the relationship. By successfully 'tension managing' in this way, men were effectively 'doing gender inequality'.
2 Conversational practices generally formed part of a discourse of woman blame, having power to locate blame for existing inequalities within the wife as an individual or the wife as a woman (i.e. problems were explained in personal or biological terms).
3 Conversational practices also had the potential to generate feelings of guilt in women by creating a version of reality in which the husband was 'hard done by' and the wife was simultaneously lucky and culpable – thereby probably compounding women's feelings of self-blame.
4 Although I am not necessarily saying that (and I have no way of knowing whether) husbands were *consciously* engaging in these undermining practices, they were nevertheless *tailoring* these woman-blaming practices to apply *personally* to their wives. Men were, therefore, participating in reflecting back

> *to their wives* a negative identity *for their wives*. I think this subtle undermining process had the power to exacerbate in women a sense of lack of confidence, low self-esteem and, in some cases, depression.

Until now, I have discussed ways in which I believe men were trying to, in Bell and Newby's (1976) terms, tension manage the opposing pulls of relational identification and gender differentiation within their relationship in order to avoid overt challenge and maintain the status quo. In the following chapter I want to continue my investigation of the interrelationship between marital identity, gender power relations and emotional experience by examining situations where men seemed to do *anything but* tension manage contradictory dimensions of their marriage. Relatedly, I will be attempting to explore what I think amounted to deep-seated tensions for some of the men I interviewed between processes of relational identity and masculinity.

5

MARITAL IDENTITY VERSUS GENDER IDENTITY – A CRISIS FOR HUSBANDS

> . . . even though size, strength, and age tend to be normally distributed among females and males (with considerable overlap between them), selective pairing ensures couples in which boys and men are visibly bigger, stronger, and older (if not 'wiser') than the girls and women with whom they are paired. So, should situations emerge in which greater size, strength, or experience is called for, boys and men will be ever ready to display it and girls and women to appreciate its display.
>
> (Goffman 1982, p. 321, quoted in West and Zimmerman 1991, p. 25)

In this chapter I want to explore some less-than-subtle practices, relating to marital identity work, gender power relations and emotional experience, engaged in by a number of the men in my interviews. I want to argue that constructions of marital identity were causing a number of problems for some of the men I talked to in the same way that subtle attempts to block change were probably becoming less effective in various cases. Practices such as those identified in Chapter 4 had the potential to do accountability work by *masking* gendered inequalities, i.e. they functioned to tension manage the contradictions between relational identification and gender differentiation. However, the feminist and liberal discourses now moving into the public domain have provided challenges to these patriarchal accounts and there was evidence in my interviews, already discussed, that women were taking up these discourses and using them to challenge – despite potential emotional and practical costs. In other words, there was evidence that some of the tension-managing practices already discussed were not working so well any more.

In Chapter 1 I borrowed West and Zimmerman's (1991) concepts of 'accountability' and 'identity work' to suggest that couples felt a keen sense of relational accountability in the interviews with me. But, of course, West and Zimmerman have used these concepts in connection with doing *gender* identity work. In what follows I want to focus simultaneously on the related concepts of marital *and* gender identity and argue that there was strong evidence in my study that men were highly resistant, within interviews, to constructing any version of reality that could significantly erode hierarchical gender difference.

Constructions of marital identity had the power to do this and were therefore a potential problem for husbands who seemed highly resistant to change.

I have divided the chapter into two main sections. The first section examines the twin concepts of relational and gender identity as connected to husbands' accounts in interviews. The second section looks more closely at the concept of gender identity, and specifically, the notion of masculinity in marriage.

Relational and gender identity: a problem for husbands

In the first section of this chapter I will, in essence, propose that if husbands were able to construct hierarchical gender difference through an emphasis on relational partnership or solidarity, they would do this. If, however, husbands were unable to define masculinity in this way, they were likely to step metaphorically outside of the notion of partnership and equality in order to reassert the 'masculine I'. First, I want to start off by looking at two examples of men who consistently defined themselves through the concept of 'we' or relational partnership throughout the interviews. Second, I will look at two examples of men who I think tended to avoid doing 'couple talk' as a way of circumventing problems of relational identification, and third I will look at examples of men who sabotaged relational identity within interviews in pursuit of the masculine 'I'.

Defining self through the relational 'we'

The first example where the man clearly defined his identity very much through the notion of partnership and solidarity with his wife was in the case of Gordon Evans. I want to focus first on extracts from Gordon's separate interview with me and, in order to fully understand some of this dialogue, it is necessary to keep in mind the point that Rachael Evans has been suffering from depression:

CAROLINE: Do you ever feel that Rachael's part of you?

GORDON: Um [pause] yes I do. [pause] It it's o– it's odd really. I, I feel – very much as if she's the sort of other half of me. You know, we're very much a sort of relationship. Partnership. And there are things, you know, there are things, which I sa– I said earlier on, well I like to be alone, but it's, always within the sort of, within the framework of the family. You – you know, you choose your moments of solitude, or whatever, or reflection, but I always find her, I mean I think I'm privileged to say that my wife is my friend as well. She is, she is my friend. And she's a great friend as well.

In this extract, Gordon gives a strong impression of partnership and equality between himself and Rachael. In the following extract – earlier in the same interview – still very much oriented around the importance of his relationship and the home and family, Gordon had this to say:

GORDON: I think she sees me as quite a stable sort of, part of her life. And I'm glad that she does, but I certainly feel, and I like to feel, that I'm a sort of fixed, and reliable, focus or point, in the sort of family. So the kids can always come to me, and and Rachael, and I'm always there and always [pause] you know, they'll get some sort of balanced treatment. I'm not sort of somebody who's – not somebody who's gonna be unpredictable, or or whatever you know. They get even, even treatment, which is I think is important.

In this extract, Gordon describes himself as a reliable focal point to whom the children and Rachael can always come, and he emphasises that 'they' – presumably the children and Rachael – get even treatment, which he thinks is important. Later on in the same interview, when discussing what makes him feel happy or good about himself he says:

GORDON: [pause] I said earlier on that I take my duties as a father very seriously, and I – that, when I see my sons happy and my wife happy [pause] I um, I feel happy, when I see them. E– like, if I, we, we went out, to take them out [pause] and to see them enjoy the trip, and enjoy, going out, we go to a restaurant, and eat, you know, they eat what they like. Um, to be interested. To show them some of the interesting things in the world, and to listen to what they have to say. That, that gives me tremendous pleasure. Um [pause] and you know, to go out, to be an interesting, it's difficult but, to be an interesting companion and partner with Rachael. To go out and enjoy things together, that, that um…yes. To feel that you're fulfilling the role as a father I s'pose, and a husband.

Once again, Gordon appears in the above extract, to be making little division between his discussion of the children and Rachael. In fact, I would argue, from these extracts and the general tenor of Gordon's separate interview, that his version of marital partnership and solidarity had a distinctly patriarchal flavour to it. In other words, I would argue that Gordon was attempting to define his masculinity through the concept of solidarity, because in so doing he could maintain a gender differentiated view of the couple and construct himself as the head of the household. In Bell and Newby's terms (1976), Gordon's account represents a classic attempt at tension management – by trying to manage simultaneously the dimensions of identification and differentiation.

It is also important to note here that Gordon, through constructing this patriarchal notion of 'we' is effectively 'doing social power'. In order to explain what I mean here I shall focus in more detail on Gordon and Rachael's biography.

Rachael, the couple told me in all three interviews, had been suffering on and off from depression since the death of her father a few years before. When her father died her mother's mental health deteriorated rapidly, and she soon became unable to look after herself. In the joint interview with Rachael and Gordon, they told me how the problem came to a head when Rachael's mother had a fall, and had to be taken to hospital with a head injury. Since that day, she had very little memory and most of the time does not even recognise Rachael. Rachael and Gordon told me that Rachael was granted power of attorney over her mother's estate, and they sold her rather large house and bought her a small flat close to their own house (her mother didn't want to move). Rachael's mother cannot do anything for herself. Rachael has to go round to the flat each morning and get her washed and dressed. Fortunately, the Social Services now provide transport every day to take her to a local day centre. She is then dropped off back at Rachael and Gordon's house in the afternoon. She stays and has tea with them and at about 8 o'clock, Gordon takes her home (Rachael cannot drive), puts her to bed and locks her in until the morning. When they had told me this, Gordon made the following comment:

GORDON: One of the things we were – we were quite concerned n– n– you know, w– wouldn't happen. W– w– we didn't want her to go to a home, because if she went into a home, what they would do, what the state would do, would be to confiscate all her [pause] her property and assets – sell them, fund the home until there was less than £3,000 left and then, you know, that would be her, well, all the things [pause] that er, her husband had, had built up over the years, would be forfeit, and we were quite determined not to let that happen. So there was, you know, a l– a number of reasons why we [pause] were prepared to put the input in. You know, we live in er, uncertain times. [laughing]. Like, we, we're blowed if we're gonna see it all sort of bl–/
CAROLINE: Blown down the
GORDON: Blown down the – you know, down the drain.
CAROLINE: Yeah, right. Gosh, that's quite a handful.
[Gordon laughs. Rachael doesn't say anything.]
[Then, later on, Gordon and Rachael are talking about their crippling schedule at the moment, with Rachael's mother and the two children:]
GORDON: But, as, as I keep saying – it's the [pause] I appreciate – we appreciate this is perhaps one of the busiest times of our lives [pause] because we've got lots of people to look after.
RACHAEL: Yeah.
GORDON: It won't always
RACHAEL: There's a lot of people dependent on us.
GORDON: Yeah, we got – we won't always be like this. We appreciate that. But in working hard now, eventually we will – gain – a certain degree of financial security. Um, and also, we are young enough at the moment and we're heal– sort of fit enough – we're young enough, to carry it off, to do it. And I, I'm quite prepared to put the input in, you know.

All the way through the above dialogue, although Rachael has said virtually nothing, Gordon has been using 'we' to describe the decision that was made to put Rachael's mother in a flat. However, later on in the same interview, Gordon has just been talking about the fact that although Rachael now gets her mother up in the mornings, he had to do it for a whole year. Rachael and Gordon then have this exchange:

RACHAEL: Yeah, I, I couldn't. That's why I was taking these tablets you see. I couldn't. When Mum went senile, you know, I mean, I just couldn't. As I went into that flat, to get her up, you know, my heart rate would go up, and I'd, not be getting panic attacks, but that sort of road, you know, that kind of avenue I could think, oh my goodness, a few more months of this and I, I, and I resented the way that I could feel that – I consciously resented the way that um [pause] you know, my, my response to Mum. I couldn't help my response to her at the time. And it was undermining me. I could feel it was undermining me and that irritated me. I thought oh I'm going down this particular road, and I – the only way I can do it is to avoid the situation. I mean, the old flight or fight thing. But I don't feel that now I mean/

GORDON: I resented that a very great – greatly at the time though because I – when [pause] when [pause] her mother did fall over in 1985, Rachael was saying oh well that's it you know. Find her a home sort of thing.

RACHAEL: Well yes I mean, I – I – we [weren't in agreement of it – really as to
GORDON: [But I was – I was...

RACHAEL: what we should do about Mum.

GORDON: And we had quite a serious, difference of opinion, but I was absolutely adamant that the [pause] the estate – should not just be, sort of wiped out...

In this extract then, I suddenly discover that the 'we' Gordon had been talking about earlier was actually him and not Rachael. In fact, at the beginning of Gordon's separate interview with me, eighteen months later, I ask him if he still thought they had done the right thing to buy the flat:

GORDON: Oh yes. If I didn't think it was the right thing it would be intolerable. I think, er, we we'd have to make a different arrangement very, very swiftly, if I felt it was the wrong thing.

In other words, Gordon is the one who is actually in the position to make such a decision. In Rachael's separate interview, she had this to say when I asked if it still felt acceptable to her that her mother wasn't in a home:

RACHAEL: Yes, it does. I mean I think initially, when we decided to do it, it was very much Gordon that took the initiative. I mean, partly because he felt – most of these homes were horrendous, and partly for sort of financial reasons really. [pause] Um I felt a bit, resentful initially. That was quite a bad period. But since we've had the tremendous support with the day care, the social services – I mean I have accepted it quite – quite happily now. I mean I don't find it a burden. I rarely feel resentful about it. Um

CAROLINE: Why did you feel resentful to start with?

RACHAEL: Well initially I felt well it's my mother and, you know, we had all this problem when my father died, I didn't know what to do with Mum, and couldn't cope with her. And we'd just had our second child [pause] and of course all that had happened when I just had Michael, the first one. I thought surely, you know, not that. After all that suffering you know, I jus– I just don't feel guilty about saying, look it's my Mum. Let's find a nice home, we can visit her three times a week. We don't have the responsibility of her care. And I felt at the time, that sort of my health and – everybody's sanity, was worth the, the money that, would be lost really. [pause] Um,but I mean I, I don't se– I mean it doesn't affect me now. We have got better at it. And it, you know, it has integrated a [pause] you know, a part of [life...

CAROLINE: [into your life

RACHAEL: Yeah, and I don't feel

CAROLINE: Yes – right.

RACHAEL: that sort of anger about it now.

Drawing the above dialogues together, although both Rachael and Gordon often talk in terms of 'we' and a sense of partnership is clearly important to both in the way they present themselves to me, the major decision concerning Rachael's mother was not a joint one. In fact it became apparent, despite Gordon's original presentation of 'we', that Rachael had strongly opposed the move. However, although it was Rachael's mother (and Rachael clearly had the major responsibility for caring for her) and despite the fact that Gordon was able to 'escape' to work whilst Rachael also had the task of caring for their two young children throughout the day – Gordon had forced through his decision. In fact, above we see him saying that if he hadn't believed it was the right thing to do he would have quickly altered the situation, whilst all Rachael can say is that she 'rarely' resents the decision now and that the anger has gone.

In speaking for both of them in this way I would suggest that Gordon's constructions of relational identity allowed him to simultaneously make a hierarchical difference between self as man and spouse as woman. Through the use of 'we', he was able to make it seem that he had Rachael's 'best interests at heart' and therefore make it extremely difficult for her to challenge. Furthermore, Rachael's recent life history had involved a series of traumas that had heightened her dependency on her husband, and had therefore restricted her range of choices for possible independent action. In fact, given these circumstances, Rachael's continuing depression could be construed in some ways as the most sensible option available in an extremely restricted set of options, a point to which I will return.

The second example where the husband seems able to construct hierarchical gender difference through the notion of marital partnership and solidarity is in the case of Gillian and Patrick Henderson. Once again, as with Rachael Evans, it is important to note here that Gillian has been suffering from depression. When I first interviewed the Hendersons, Gillian had given birth to their third child only three weeks before. She told me in the second interview, eighteen months later, that she was extremely depressed after the birth and had only in recent months started to feel better. In the following extract from their joint interview, Patrick constructs a similar, rather patriarchal view of Gillian and the children:

CAROLINE: Could you say how similar or different you are?
PATRICK: I think we're, I think we're very different really, don't you?
GILLIAN: [pause] I'd say he's much calmer than me. I – I am the one that worries and – gets in a state and [pause]/
PATRICK: Oh I can sort of turn aggression on and off if I need to [pause] get things changed. [pause] But, sort of remain in control.
CAROLINE: Mm.
[pause]
GILLIAN: Not with me [laughing a bit].
PATRICK: Not, not with you no but – no – sort of to protect the family if you like, or whatever. Yeah, most of the time I'm a very calm person.
GILLIAN: [pause] Er, very confident, self-reliant I guess.
[pause]
PATRICK: I dunno. I assume that's how you see me [laughing a bit].
GILLIAN: [slight laugh] Yes [very quietly].

In this extract it is interesting to notice how Gillian, in saying 'not with me' in response to Patrick saying he can turn aggression on and off to remain in control, is effectively articulating the romantic Mills and Boon idea of relational identification transcending inequalities. Patrick concurs with her depiction but – in a similar way to Gordon Evans – sets himself aside slightly from Gillian and the children by talking about the way in which he protects them. Later on in the interview, I asked Patrick and Gillian if they felt they influenced each other at all:

PATRICK: [slight laugh] I like to think that I get you to do things, which you should do.
CAROLINE: Can you give me an example?
PATRICK: Yeah. A good example is um [pause] there's an atrocious midwife in [the village]. Well, she's a a – very nice lady you know. I'd certainly go to the shop and have a chat with her if she was a shop keeper but as a midwife she's hopeless! You know. I've had this opinion and so have you – and half the village – ever since our first baby, and Gillian said that she

didn't want the midwife. Um, having decided that, you know, I said 'you must write a letter to the doctor or whatever and make sure you don't get her'. And you weren't gonna do that. And I [pause] not insisted, but I put pressure on you to do that. You know, I'd like to [pause] you know I think that people are sort of trodden on. You know, that people are too nice sometimes and that – you were gonna put up with this woman, who was absolutely hopeless and made you nervous, when she did things to the baby like [pause] take blood and things, you know, had you shaking. You know. You put up with that because you didn't wanna hurt her feelings or embarrass the doctor, and I [pause] said now forget it, and [pause] that's most important [pointing to the baby], you're next important and the doctor can be embarrassed and say that you don't want this woman. And lo and behold [pause] you know, you got – wrote this letter, pursued it, got all these names out of people, took their numbers and arranged it, and it was – it was – wasn't it? [he laughs slightly] So I mean, you know, I think I do, influence you in that way.

Gillian replied to Patrick's comments by saying that 'he's a great one for making her stand up for herself'. However, it is interesting to note that all through his speech I made the usual polite 'mm' noises in pauses but Gillian said absolutely nothing. In fact, later in the discussion, I came back to this question to ask Gillian in what way she felt she influenced Patrick:

GILLIAN: [pause] [laughing awkwardly] I don't really – I don't know [laughing] – I don't think I've got any.

CAROLINE: Perhaps you should think about that and come…

PATRICK: Yes.

CAROLINE: It's really difficult to ask people things like that I mean/

PATRICK: Well that's right I mean these are the questions we haven't really asked ourselves even.

CAROLINE: That's right, and I think also I'm aware as well that you could um – think one thing – I could think one thing about that one minute and another thing the next.

PATRICK: Mm.

GILLIAN: I should think it's probably, the in– influence I have is [pause] you know, the old fashioned one of, you know that [pause] if you see I'm upset or whatever, you will give in or [pause] you know, make allowances or whatever.

[pause]

CAROLINE: Mm.

GILLIAN: Which is not how it should be. [she and I laugh a bit]. Very – very old fashioned isn't it.

PATRICK: Oh yeah I think – I think it's terrible, yeah I do [laughing]. True though.

As is probably obvious from my above contribution to the discussion, I found this exchange very difficult and did not know what to say. Although Gillian laughed when she said she did not think she had any influence, she seemed awkward and embarrassed. Furthermore, I felt that I was in some sense colluding with Patrick by pushing this issue, a point to which I will return later.

One of the recurring issues in discussions with Patrick and Gillian was their differing views about family obligations. Gillian felt that they should take some responsibility for caring for parents and other people while Patrick took the view that allegiance should be to the nuclear family only. In this joint interview, Gillian's concern about relatives becomes translated by Patrick as a tendency for her to be 'put upon'. Patrick is, however, able to impose his definition of events through the notion of family unity. For example, in the following extract, he says:

PATRICK: [slight laugh] Yeah and I think basic– men are – will impose and women don't, but er [pause] [slight laugh] it does seem to be you've been brought up to [pause] you know, think of other people, you know. I've been brought up to sort of go out and get what I want, I s'pose, but now I'm – sort of applying it for us.

Finally, at the end of this interview, I asked Gillian and Patrick what love meant to them. Gillian said it wasn't about infatuation. Patrick had this to say:

PATRICK: I think it's more of a union isn't it – a sort of mental [pause] union – whereas I mean I [pause] I know really what you want, and you know what I'm thinking or – the sort of you know – how I want my life to go – that sort of thing. And er [pause] you know, we sort of know – what to do for each other. But er…

CAROLINE: Mmm…a mental [union.

PATRICK: [No, it's – literally [pause] you know, we're not sort of separate people any more really.

In sum, to draw these two accounts together, I would argue that both Patrick Henderson and Gordon Evans were able to define a sense of differentiated masculinity *through* a construction of relational *romantic* identification. I have attempted to illustrate above the ways in which I believe both these men, through defining the couple in this way, were 'doing gendered power relations'. For Gordon, conceptually homogenising the couple served to prevent Rachael from challenging his decision with regard to her mother. For Patrick, amalgamating the couple served to protect his hold on the marital agenda because his action was constructed as 'for them' and not for him. Perhaps Patrick's concept of mental union could more usefully be renamed 'mental takeover'.

Stepping into hierarchical gender difference

In this section I want to examine two examples in joint accounts where husbands appeared to step into an account of hierarchical gender difference by mistake whilst discussing their relationships, thus creating a potential challenge to the notion of relational partnership and solidarity. It is worth reiterating at this point that the interviews often presented rather novel situations for husbands and wives to talk about issues perhaps not usually discussed. This could create problems for husbands who perhaps were not used to talking much about aspects of their relationship or who had perhaps used silence or 'remoteness' before in the relationship as a way of avoiding conflict. The following two extracts are taken from conversations with couples where, in each case, the husband appears to be unaccustomed to having these kinds of conversation with his wife. (The first husband is in a middle-class occupation and the second husband in a working-class occupation.) The first example is from the joint account of Nick and Sally Freeman.

Almost at the end of the interview with the Freemans I ask:

CAROLINE: Generally, more generally, in relation to men and women, do you think that there's equality nowadays, not necessarily just in marriage but…

SALLY: Not really no. There's still a lot of areas aren't there where there's er [pause] a lot of inequality I think.

CAROLINE: What sort of areas would you?

SALLY: Well most of the professions, I mean there's still the – it's still difficult for women to get into a lot of professions isn't it – I mean with this business about, you know, me having to go back to work full-time, for instance, you see. If I went into nurse teaching – now if I was a man and I was a breadwinner – no problem you see. Um [pause] so that's one example. I dunno what it – what's it like with teaching? Is it er?

NICK: Oh I mean subconscious – well not even subconsciously I mean if – if there's a, you know, a job going – senior post, or senior job, I mean if – if a woman got the job, you know, I think I'm sure I'd tend to think 'ooh, she's not gonna be very strong' – that sort of thing.

CAROLINE: Mm, mm.

NICK: I mean so there's that, sort of prejudice there, you know, however I behave, you know, towards it. And um…

SALLY: Oh I didn't know [that. Would you really?

NICK: [Oh yes Oh I think – I but I mean I'd be aware of it I mean that's [been my reaction probably yes.

SALLY: [Would you? Would it really? [looking uncomfortable]

NICK: Oh yeah.

SALLY: I didn't know that. [pause] So I mean what about things like, women doctors and – women dentists and things like that – would you feel – um, reluctant to consult/

NICK: Well I – no, I s'pose I'm, er more used to, er, seeing more of those. No I – no I haven't really come across many sort of, headmistresses and – I've not worked under headmistresses really. [pause] So maybe that's it, that's why – why I think that way. Partly anyway. But I'm sure there's, you know [obscured by Sally rustling in the ironing bag and appearing stressed].

CAROLINE: Do you think it – it's to do with [I say this to placate] sort of getting used to the idea then?

SALLY: Yeah, it is and it's to do with/

NICK: Probably yeah I mean I don't think um [pause] I'd resent it, you know, it's not a case of resenting it once it was established um.

In the final few lines, above, I actually add a comment to try to defuse the tension and my comment does indeed seem to have this effect. However, the main point here is that Sally had to face Nick saying in the interview that he would probably be prejudiced about a female headmistress, and tend to think she wouldn't be strong enough. Sally challenges Nick on this and he reverses his position slightly. But I would argue that it was still a particularly uncomfortable moment for Sally – and Nick – particularly in view of the fact that she had just finished telling me about the importance of her own career for her feelings of self-worth, and talking about the inequality that women still suffer in the labour market.

The second example I want to look at here is quite similar to Sally and Nick's account. This is an extract, once again, from Sarah and Malcolm Anderson:

MALCOLM: Well, from my point of view, I'd consider it feminine, being like Sarah is, running a house, although maybe that's wrong, you know, but er [pause] well an – keeping herself smart and that in'it I mean, at the moment where I'm working at [company] there's women there doing – blokes' work if you like um [pause] well, big business women if you like and I find that a bit of a turn off in some ways. You know, ah/

SARAH: Uh [slight humorous exclamation of indignation]. Just as well isn't it! [laughing and then me laughing]

MALCOLM: No but they – they come in and talk to to you [pause] as your equal.

SARAH: Sort of like man to man?

MALCOLM: And they sort of push you in a corner whereas, the roles used to seem, a bit different like you kn– not that I want a woman to be under me thumb.

CAROLINE: Mm.

MALCOLM: But er [pause] ooh what – well, they're a threat then [slight laugh] if you like, in a way you know.

CAROLINE: Yeah.

In the above extract, Malcolm has actually gone so far as to say the problem with women at his workplace is that they talk to him like his equal. Sarah appears to try to 'translate' this as 'sort of like man to man?' He ignores her comment but starts to move from his original position to say that perhaps the problem is that these women seem like a threat. The conversation continues:

MALCOLM: Um maybe that's wrong. I don't know, because of, you know, I've got old fashioned views on that, probably. But um, good luck to a woman that can get on with a career and that but er [pause] they're not just equal sort of thing though, they seem to be – a bit over and above that like and I don't – consider that as feminine, you know, really.
SARAH: Perhaps [it's because they're female that they feel they have to
MALCOLM: [I don't.
SARAH: you know, prove themselves.

At this stage, Malcolm is implying that maybe the problem is that inequality has swung too far the other way and it is now hard on men. I pointed out earlier that quite a few men in my study did this. In fact, the conversation continues:

MALCOLM: Well yeah, I s'pose this is it. A– for anybody who's been oppressed, and I s'pose women 'ave been for a long time – by being given the standard role and, looked down on, you know, the– their coming back and coming back strong, you know. Um [pause] but er – I find them coming on a little bit heavy, you know, at times um.

Malcolm appears at this stage to be trying to reconstruct himself to Sarah and me as 'enlightened' – i.e. the original comment about equality was a slip of the tongue – and saying merely that the problem is these women are 'coming on a bit strong'. It's fair enough that they are wanting to prove themselves because they have been 'oppressed', and 'given the standard role and, looked down on'. The point I want to make here is that, superficially, this last comment is more egalitarian than Malcolm's first, that women talk to him like an equal and he finds this 'a bit of a turn off'. However, I would suggest that the impact of the last comment is almost harder for Sarah to accept than the first. In fact, at this point in the conversation, she went completely quiet, leaving Malcolm to answer my questions. This is not surprising: it is not just that Malcolm has suggested that the women where he works should not treat him as an equal. In back-pedalling from this position, he has stated that women have been 'oppressed, given the standard role and looked down on', and yet they have both told me that Sarah has the 'standard role'. What is Malcolm then saying about Sarah? Does he look down on her? Is he 'oppressing' her? At the end of the visit, I ask them how they found the interview:

SARAH: Nobody ever asks me what I'd like [laughing] so it's quite unusual really, you know, it's quite nice for us it, sort of clarifies it in your own mind, what you are doing you know.

MALCOLM: It draws things, it draws thing, you're drawing things out of us saying about each other that – we wouldn't normally say, you know. Probably, as I said, taking each other for granted and that like, [you know so um.
SARAH: [Yeah, you think, you prhaps think the other, realises and maybe they don't, you know. It can make a lot of difference really.
CAROLINE: So has anything that either of you said, sort of surprised the other one or [pause] Do you know what I mean?
SARAH: [pause] What, this evening?
CAROLINE: Well yes, or either time really.
SARAH: Um [pause] [cautiously] I think Malcolm's a bit chauvinistic with these women in – industry and one thing and another [laughing a bit and me laughing].
MALCOLM: No – well, you might have got me wrong there no [we're still laughing]. Um.
SARAH: Yeah, I thi– I found that a bit surprising you know.
MALCOLM: Mm.
SARAH: Not, not ever so really. Nothing apart from that I don't think really.
MALCOLM: Mm. No, it wasn't a case of being chauvinistic but I mean, well I feel with a diff– a lot of different women sort of work in – well from nurses, to sisters and one thing and another, and I see different attitudes. Well, in hospitals they, they've got a high position, but their attitude is different to what they are in say something like, well like [place where he works] like, you know.
SARAH: Yeah.
MALCOLM: Um, I wasn't being chauvinistic at all about it, but then, that's a cross section of women and – blokes vary the same don't they, you know?
SARAH: Oh yeah.
CAROLINE: Mm.
MALCOLM: An' – um – [yeah. I wasn't being chauvinistic really.
SARAH: [I'll let you off that one [we all laugh].

To draw these two examples together, I would suggest that it is quite likely that Malcolm and Nick made their original comments 'without really thinking'. Furthermore, their comments are likely to have been experienced as oppressive and disempowering by their wives. In short, their comments cut straight through the protective conceptual barrier that most spouses were using when they told me that inequality wasn't an issue in their own relationship.

Malcolm and Nick's action, however, in stepping so obviously into an account of hierarchical gender difference, had the effect of making them accountable to their wives for their comments. They both had to retract their original statements and in fact Malcolm, at the end of their interview, had to answer the charge of chauvinism from Sarah. Furthermore, these particular examples illustrate the point that such comments could occur whether the husband described himself as 'traditional' and 'old fashioned' – as in the case of Malcolm – or where the husband described himself as 'enlightened' and talked about the ways in which gender inequality was essentially a problem for people who had not had the advantage of a good education, as in the case of Nick.

There are some difficult implications in these two extracts for the meaning-making aspects of relational identity. Malcolm and Nick's 'slips' shed considerable doubt on the idea that close relational identification is transcending social inequalities in terms of relational 'meaning-making' with these husbands. In a nutshell, both these extracts could be read as suggesting that Malcolm and Nick think their wives are essentially inferior to them and that relational identification, in their eyes, is hierarchically structured. Examples such as the above also demonstrate how talking about a relationship might present considerable difficulties to a man who thinks in this way. During discussions, Malcolm frequently seemed to 'tie himself up in knots' of the kind outlined above while Nick was generally 'low key' to the point of being monosyllabic at various stages in the interviews – in other words he tended to withdraw. Silence or physical distancing (e.g. spending a lot of time away from partner) can be good strategies for deflecting challenge and I will return to this point later.

Redefining separate identity

In this section I want to argue that, for most of the men I interviewed, it was becoming harder and harder to construct relational identification through either hierarchical gender difference or silence. Wives' changing aspirations, as evidenced in the interviews, meant that relational definitions were probably being challenged on a day-to-day basis with most of the couples I interviewed. The interviews the couples participated in also formed, at one level, a part of women's changing aspirations for heterosexual relationships. I raised issues with the couples born out of my own beliefs and aspirations and the interview provided a good forum for debating feminist ideas. Some of the couples had voluntarily contacted me to participate in the study and laid themselves open to just such discussions. Although neither the Freemans nor the Andersons had voluntarily contacted me, both of the above extracts contain traces of feminist discourses – e.g. when Malcolm states that women have been oppressed, or when Nick acknowledges that his views might amount to 'prejudice'.

Yet, despite all this, *the fact is* there was strong evidence of a reluctance amongst the men in my study to countenance change. In particular, I think that several of the men I interviewed were having difficulty in controlling the marital agenda and were confused and unhappy that they seemed unable to *block change*. Therefore, in order to try to protect themselves from the implications of potential changes in the relationship, they were psychologically distancing themselves from their wives and, in many cases, their children as well. I will attempt to demonstrate what I mean here by focusing on dialogue from separate interviews with Richard Price, Peter Docherty and Mike Walters respectively – men who all seemed particularly unhappy with the nature of family life as they experienced it:

CAROLINE: What do you feel is really important to you in life for you to feel good about yourself, and happy?

RICHARD: Oh blimey.

CAROLINE: [laughing a bit] 10 million dollar question.

RICHARD: Yeah. Um [pause] Well in my case it's it's, purely to do with work. I feel good about me if I've had a – or if my [job] has gone well, and this year as I say, I've been to these shows and I've done well and, so that has, yeah, I'm very confident that what I'm doing as a job I'm very very good at. And um, so that's made me feel good about myself yeah. That's workwise. Um [pause] Home life I don't know. I mean I – can't really relate it to home. [pause] If we get through the day having had a good happy day, and then we all go to bed and wake up feeling happy I s'pose, that makes you feel good but, yeah, certainly workwise it's going well.

In the same way, when I asked Peter Docherty the same question, he replied:

PETER: Um [pause] I guess I think I value probably respect of others [pause] for [pause] what you do, what you know and what you deliver, certainly in terms of the job. Um [pause] er, I've always tried to be – helpful towards other people you kno– whether it's at work or [pause] jus– around. I like to help and be part of things that are going on. Um, certainly at work people look on me as a repository if they want to find something or know something, they tend to come to me and say, where is this or how do I do that? and I like that.

[He continues in this vein and then he says:]

PETER: So for me I guess satisfaction at work is very important. Um [pause] and the things that gives you in terms of [pause] self-satisfaction – the money side usually enables you to do all the other things that you wanna do.

He carries on for a while talking about his job, and then I turn the tape over. When I turn the tape back on he appears to still be pondering this issue of feeling good and happy about self, for he says:

PETER: I'm trying to think if there's anything else but I mea– there is quite a lot of things I guess but, those are the main things. I'm a very work biased person. Maybe other people give you answers about home and [pause] things like that – maybe it's more important to them. Um – I tend to think if you're doing well in that environment, as an individual you're content and [pause] the rewards from that and the money tend to enable you to [laughing a bit] [pause] do the rest of the things yeah.

The important point to be drawn from the above two extracts is that both Peter and Richard have suggested that they cannot actively relate this question to the home sphere. This domain is presented as outside of what is important to them – or outside of a sense of who they really are. In the same way, Mike Walters seems keen, at points in his separate interview, to distance himself from 'the wife and kids'. He emphasises that he and Liz have quite separate existences and that they don't talk very much. In fact, he tells me that he talks more to his 'mate' at work than he does to 'the wife':

MIKE: And er [pause] I think I could talk to him about more or less anything. Er, not that I do, but I feel that I could. Because we work together all the time. We both do exactly the same job. What he can't do, I have to. What I can't do, he has to do. So we don't have to look after each other's tail. But we're always in, intimate contact. We– I see more of him than I see of the wife. So I guess in a way, he's the one you have to talk to really and he's, very good.

Mike, in this account, is effectively counteracting a notion of a close heterosexual partnership in which spouse equals best friend, by saying that he is closer to his workmate than his wife.

In sum, I have used the above extracts to illustrate ways in which some of the men in my study – far from constructing a sense of relational *romantic* identity in interviews, seemed to be metaphorically separating themselves from a wife and children and redefining a separate identity. I think that what was going on here was much more than simply that these particular husbands were not happy at home. In the following section, I want to stay with Peter, Richard and Mike and examine how this process seemed to translate into joint interview interaction.

Sabotaging relational identity

In joint interviews with their wives, Richard, Peter and Mike all constructed an account of distance – this time directly from the concept of couple in dialogue with their wives. The following extract may be familiar from the very beginning of this book:

CAROLINE: Do you, in terms of doing things, you know, in terms of cooking and cleaning and gardening, stuff like that, are there particular things that one of you do that the other one wouldn't or, how do you organise/
RICHARD: Yes...cook.
MARGARET: Cooking, I do all the cooking.
RICHARD: But nearly everything else [pause] it's/

MARGARET: In the house Richard'll – I mean Richard's put the hoover round this morning. Um, yes, you'll clean the bath and yes, he does everything round the house 'cept cooking. I do the ironing. I tend to do the ironing.
RICHARD: I don't iron.
MARGARET: [pause] Yeah you say 'I don't iron!' like as if, well, I shouldn't have to iron, but it's only – you could if you put your mind to it.
RICHARD: That's – what I meant [laughing a bit like 'oh dear']. No, I don't iron and I don't cook. (a) cause I wouldn't enjoy ironing and there's no way I'm gonna do that and (b) [pause] er cooking I'm, I'm/
MARGARET: Why do you say there's no way I'm gonna do that?
RICHARD: I don't wanna be standing there with an iron. No thank you.
MARGARET: Fine! [pause] Tomorrow you do the ironing.
[I laugh awkwardly and alone. The atmosphere has become tense.]

I used this extract at the outset of this book to raise some preliminary questions concerning what dialogue such as the above could mean. At this point in the book I hope my interpretation of the multi-layered, complex sub-text of such dialogue is becoming more obvious. In particular, I think that in this extract:

- Margaret and Richard start off here constructing a relational identity that incorporates modern, democratic and feminist values of gender undifferentiated sharing.
- Richard panics as the ensuing construction of reality erodes his sense of his own masculinity. They are together painting a picture he might have to live.
- He sacrifices the developing account of relational equality in order to reassert the masculine 'I' by (1) trying to demonstrate that he, unlike his wife, has the power to determine which household chores he will and won't do and (2) trying to position ironing as 'work not for him'.
- In sacrificing the developing account of relational equality he becomes 'accountable' to Margaret for his action. She picks him up on the sub-text that it is 'work not for him' when she says 'why do you say there's no way I'm gonna do that?' and then directly challenges his version of events by saying 'Fine…tomorrow you do the ironing.'

The main point here is not just that Richard is trying to show that he has the power to select what he will and won't do in the house. An important sub-text of this dialogue then is that Richard seems to be implying here that ironing is beneath him, for example, when he says, 'I don't wanna be standing there with an iron'. This point links back to the argument I developed in Chapter 4, that men often gave the impression that although they could 'technically' carry out the tasks for which their wives were responsible, in practice they would not really be able to do this work because it was 'women's work', and consequently 'slightly inferior'. I would suggest that this 'hidden implication' is clearly what is bothering Margaret when she says 'why do you say there's no way I'm gonna do that?'

In sum, then, I think what is happening in this extract is that the version of relational identity being constructed is a threat to, rather than a vehicle for, Richard doing hierarchical gender difference. Richard therefore sacrifices relational accountability to, as it were, reassert the masculine 'I'. In order to underline this point, I would like to move on to Peter Docherty's joint account with his wife. In the following extract, I would suggest that Joan Docherty is concerned to present a relatively egalitarian account to me around overall division of labour. However, Peter appears to want to do the opposite:

CAROLINE: Who does the cooking at weekends?
[pause]
JOAN: We split it between us really.
PETER: Mm [as in – maybe].
JOAN: We always have done [laughing slightly].
PETER: [We don't think about it really I mean/
JOAN: [I tend – I tend to cook Sunday lunch [shouting him down]. [pause] Um [pause] I don't know why I – well, I say cook it, I'll put it in the oven. There's not a lot to do is there. Um, yeah we split it between us. There's no particular conscious, effort, if it's getting towards one o'clock and I've made no move, Peter'll get up and say what – [drowned out by him laughing] It depends really what we're having [having to talk really loud to be heard over him laughing], if it's something that needs preparing and I have to buy in all the ingredients and what have you then I'll cook it but – if it's – as it often is on a Saturday, we – if we've got – and we have French bread and cheese and pâté and what have you, then it's, you know, he'll get up and put it out on the table as likely as I would.

The overall effect of Peter's doubtful 'maybe' combined with his peal of laughter in the middle of Joan's account, is to undermine what she is saying and give the impression that he doesn't help at all at the weekends – which is actually what Joan says on different occasions. And in fact, even Joan's above account suggests that Peter's 'help' is minimal. However, the major issue at this juncture is not whether Peter really does put the cheese and pâté on the table at weekends. Rather, Joan clearly wants to construct events in this way to me here, and Peter seems to be fighting her construction. I would argue, as with Richard Price above, that what Peter is actually doing here is sabotaging relational accountability because the relational identity being constructed is too much of an erosion of hierarchical gender difference. Furthermore, the version of everyday life Joan is constructing here is one that Peter may have to live in future if he is not careful.

The final example I would like to give here is from the joint account of Liz and Mike Walters. In this account, once again, the couple have been telling me who does what around the house. In this extract, they are both working from a 'breadwinner–homemaker' agenda:

CAROLINE: Can I ask you, generally, who does what? Do you [to her] – who cooks?

LIZ: Yes.

CAROLINE: I mean, in general, do you find that, because you go to work [to him] or you have children [to her] that you tend to/

LIZ: Yeah.

CAROLINE: You do the housework and...

LIZ: Yes.

MIKE: Occasionally, I do – something towards the cooking. I peel the spuds or the carrots on Sunday/

LIZ: Like if I get up first thing on a Sunday morning and put all the vegetables, that I'm going to cook, in the bowl, and then go upstairs and get in the [bath for an hour.

MIKE: [She leaves them out so I – Yeah [she and I laugh]. They get peeled.
[all laughing]

LIZ: I wait until I hear the dustbin lid! [laughing]

CAROLINE: And then you get out of the bath.

LIZ: And then I know the vegetables are done.
[pause]

LIZ: That's probably about the extent of it.

MIKE: Yeah.

LIZ: Or, Saturdays, I mean [pause] a snack at lunch time – sausage and chips then, Mike's/

MIKE: I'll do that. [Yeah, I can turn the chip pan on. Simple really!

LIZ: [I mean it's not that – it's not necessarily that he can't do it. It's just [that

MIKE: [I don't need to. I've got a wife! [laughing, and I laugh awkwardly]

LIZ: Oh that's not fair [not laughing]. [suppressed laughter from him] Yes, it's just that I'm here and...

CAROLINE: Yeah.

As with the two other examples above, we see the now familiar pattern of the husband sacrificing a construction of relational equality to reassert the masculine 'I'. In so doing he, along with Richard and Peter above, are constructing oppressive versions of reality that are less than subtle.

To draw these accounts together, I would argue that it would be impossible for the women in these interviews to pass such comments off as 'not about our relationship' as was potentially possible in the case of Sally Freeman and Sarah Anderson discussed earlier in the chapter. Men in the above examples were obviously talking about their own relationship when they stepped out of equity and tried to assert their superiority as a man. These exchanges, I would argue, were likely to be particularly distressing for the wives concerned. It was impossible here for them to redraw successfully the boundary between the intergroup and the interpersonal, once the husband had broken it. Furthermore, I would suggest that, particularly in the case of Liz Walters, Mike was likely to have been expressing her worst fear. It is worth noting that Mike tries to pass off the comment in a fairly jokey way. However, Liz does not treat the comment as a joke. I would argue that this is because the comment touches a raw nerve. Consider the following extract (partially reproduced in Chapter 1) from my separate interview with Liz:

CAROLINE: Do you think marriage has changed?
LIZ: Definitely [long pause] a more equal partnership than when the wife used to stay at home, all day.
CAROLINE: Is that true of your marriage?
LIZ: Yes, I think so. We both do an equal amount.
[…]
CAROLINE: Do you think that um, thinking about men and women in general, do you think that there is equality between men and women?
LIZ: In what way?
CAROLINE: Well, in any way. Not just in/
LIZ: Equality?
CAROLINE: Equality
LIZ: Yes, there is. I mean [longish pause] there's much more, much more men going into, to women's jobs and vice v– you know. I mean, there's more, you know, girls that can have that. And that's how it should be! [both laugh] really.
CAROLINE: So you think it's equal?
LIZ: It's – getting [there, it's getting there.
CAROLINE: [It's on the way
LIZ: Whether or not it will ever be [pause] fully equal I can't really say.
[…]
LIZ: I suppose men have always been the provider. So [long pause] and women have always been, they've always been subservient really haven't they, and I think, men have always, been the dominant ones.
CAROLINE: Do you think that's/
LIZ: It's [longish pause] it's ongoing [longish pause]. Er – it's changing. But they still are, really. They still like to think they are anyway! I mean, whether or not there's a strong woman underneath every man?!

In the above extract, Liz moves from a depiction of marriage as an equal partnership through to marriage as a hierarchical relation of dominance and subservience. She constructs both versions, yet through the use of the 'general' (i.e. 'they' rather than 'he' and 'I') she manages the tension between these opposing versions of reality. However, in the joint dialogue transcribed above, Mike has effectively brought these two dimensions together, creating, I would suggest, what is likely to have been a less than pleasant experience for Liz. In fact, Mike reinforces this hierarchical construction of reality later in the same interview when he tells Liz and I that 'the father should be boss of his own house'.

In sum, in this chapter so far I have tried to demonstrate ways in which I think men in my study group were trying to construct *hierarchical* gender difference within interview conversations. I have further tried to outline ways in which I think constructions of relational identity became, as it were, 'victims' to this cause at various points. If constructions of relational identity could not incorporate hierarchical gender difference, they were avoided or sabotaged by husbands. The relational identities being fashioned by wives, therefore, had the potential to end up rather lonely or distressing places – a metaphorical 'wilderness' at the crossroads of a marriage. I will continue this theme in Chapter 6.

Masculinity and marriage

> He laughed insolently, triumphantly. Undoing another button of his shirt, he lounged out across the yard to the shed where Big Business, the bull, was imprisoned in darkness. Laughing softly, Seth struck the door of the shed. And as though answering the deep call of male to male, the bull uttered a loud tortured bellow that rose undefeated through the dead sky that brooded over the farm. Seth undid yet another button, and lounged away.
>
> (Stella Gibbons, *Cold Comfort Farm*, 1932, p. 42)

In the third part of this chapter I want to stay with the problem of hierarchical gender difference and focus specifically on some particularly problematic aspects of masculinity construction in my data.

It is important to note at this stage that, by sabotaging their wives' accounts of equity and asserting masculinity, Mike, Richard and Patrick were all implicitly constructing an image of their wives. I pointed out earlier that, amongst other reasons, women were likely to be trying to present an equitable view of their relationship to me because such a construction of reality would be 'face saving', in Goffman's terms. Men, in breaking out of a joint construction of fairness were likely to be sabotaging this version of reality for their wives. But more than this, an extremely important point to be underlined here is that the very essence of masculinity, as constructed in such accounts, appeared to be about oppressing women. Mike Walters tried to look 'macho' through implying that his wife was a servant. Richard Price did the same by suggesting that certain tasks that his wife did were beneath him. Peter Docherty conveyed the impression, by laughing throughout his wife's construction of equity, that she waited on him, but not vice versa. In fact, in his separate interview, Peter Docherty said at one stage: 'sounds like she does everything, she probably does!' I would argue that his wife's domestic servicing 'overload' was being presented to me by Peter as a show of his own strength. In the rest of this chapter, I want to look a bit more closely at the rather sinister underside of husbands' constructions of masculinity in marriage. The section is divided into three parts.

Masculinity, husbands and 'not being pushed around'

There was a marked tendency in my interviews for men to try to convey to me the impression that no-one told them what to do, or tried to 'push them around'. Such a stance often emerged in relation to home maintenance, a task which most spouses claimed to be the responsibility of the men. For example, in the following extract from a joint interview with Carol and Tony Matthews, we had been discussing this topic and Tony had been emphasising how much he enjoyed such work. However, in this extract, Carol begins by telling me that home maintenance is actually an area of disagreement between the couple because Tony won't do it. Tony, in this extract, constructs an account of why he won't do it, where he explains that his reason was due to Carol's behaviour. He had therefore decided to 'put his foot down':

CAROLINE: Do you have, many disagreements about anything – and if so what?
CAROL: Um [pause] well we do have rows don't we? – occasionally.
TONY: Oh yeah – occasionally.
[pause]
CAROL: I dunno. What do we argue about?
TONY: Ah there you are see – it must be trifling.
CAROLINE: [laughing] You can't remember!
TONY: I can't remember [laughing].
CAROL: I get me hair off cause the house is in such a state [pause] and then I give up, cause the more I keep on, the less he will do [she laughs].
TONY: You found that out with the bathroom didn't you?
CAROL: [pause] Yeah, this had been waiting for sort of six months to be done and he'd got hold of this bathroom suite from his friend
TONY: No no no no. I'm [talking about way way before that!
CAROL: [Oh – What?
TONY: Let me think. I think it was when we only had Jane.
CAROL: That's bloody [pause] ages ago.
TONY: When I started tiling the bathroom.
CAROL: Yeah?

TONY: I put some tiles round the bathroom – started a row off – started a row off, along the other wall, and I started from the next lot then in the corner, going the other way – Carol gets bored very easily, don't you?

CAROL: Yeah.

TONY: [pause] And whereas um – usually when I start a job [pause] I usually – cause I, I think I was working at the time [pause] or was I? I can't remember. Usually, if I, if I've started a job, any spare moment I've got I start on it. So soon as I come home, instead of sitting down and having me tea, get on with it. [pause] And weekends as well. Soon as I get up in the morning, before I have breakfast, get on with it like you know? And Carol gets bored easily – and um [pause] used to turn round and say – I'm bored I wanna go out.

CAROL: Oh yeah. [laughing] Oh yeah I'm like that [laughing].

TONY: So I say right, fair enough. I said I'm busy. No, I wanna go out. So that's it. Put my tools down. Leave it exactly like it is.

CAROL: And then I get me 'air off cause it isn't done.

TONY: And then we go out [pause] and I think right – sod it, that can stay there. And that bathroom got left, with a few tiles on that wall and a few tiles along this, for three years.

CAROLINE: Three years! [laughing]

TONY: Three years it was like it. And it was a talking point of everybody that came to the house. 'Has he finished that tiling yet?'

CAROL: Yeah.

TONY: Has he finished that tiling? Not that I didn't do anything else. Cause a couple of months later I'd pick up me tools and I'd start somewhere else in the house.

CAROL: That's what he does. He starts things, and he doesn't finish them. That's the thing. That's what I – get annoyed about.

TONY: Yeah but – it was only for the fact that – you said that you were bored and wanted to go out. You wouldn't give me a chance to finish it! I left the bathroom – purposely – for three years. After a couple of months I started other jobs – I just left the bathroom. It looked bloody awful!
[pause]

CAROLINE: Is it done now?

TONY: Oh yeah. It didn't worry me. [pause] It didn't worry me at all [pause].

CAROL: I worry [more than you though.

TONY: [And then eventually, because I got, Carol got fed up with – moaning about it, and either, everybody that used to come here used to moan about it – and I purposely/

CAROLINE: Left it.

TONY: And then when I, when I fancied doing it, I went up there, and I finished it, as good as gold. All in one go. Cause Carol knew, if she moaned at me again, said I want to go out, it'd stay there another three years [I laugh unconvincingly].

Although, in the middle of this extract, Carol attempts another perspective – that Tony never finishes work that he starts – Tony constructs a justification for leaving the task for three years by claiming that the whole thing was Carol's fault (i.e. because she has 'moaned' at him). The extract also reflects the point that while most couples I interviewed said that home maintenance was the husband's task, the ultimate worry about the appearance of the home rested on the woman's shoulders. However, the main point I want to make here is that in the last paragraph of the construction, Tony metaphorically appears to 'flex his masculine muscles'. He would do the job when he was good and ready and if it took Carol three years to 'learn her lesson', then so be it. The implication in the last line is that, if Carol learns to 'behave', she will get her way.

Other men told me similar stories about 'not liking to be pushed', particularly in relation to home maintenance. For example, Gordon Evans in a separate interview, when I asked him if there was anything Rachael encouraged him to do, told me that:

GORDON: I don't think she – she doesn't really get on to me about anything. Doing chores around the house – I mean, I do that. But actually I don't like being sort of – poked into things, that's me. I hate that. Goaded in, I mean, I'm gonna do something, I do it. I don't want somebody – and if I'm in the middle of doing something I don't wanna be told there's something else I should be doing as well, cause that just gets me you know [I laugh] – gets to me [he laughs a bit]. Got a thing about that.

CAROLINE: Can that cause sort of disagreements then or?

GORDON: Oh yeah – yeah, I mean I start, that's when I start flaring up a bit you know. That really does, that rattles my cage a lot, that does.

CAROLINE: And does, do those sorts of things, do those kind of disagreements last very long or?

GORDON: No.

CAROLINE: They blow over.

GORDON: I'll go and be in a huff for twenty minutes. I can be extremely rude and have been extremely rude, and then I, you know, you know, when you're being rude and [pause] [sigh] I always say sorry. That's the only way to proceed I think.

Sometimes, comments in the above vein seemed to be made in the interview situation very much for the sake of presentation per se. I felt that what men were actually doing was trying to assert themselves within the conversation. So, for example, Peter Docherty, in his separate interview, says that:

PETER: – One thing Joan hates about me is that I don't argue. I consider it to be a waste of time but I think she'd love to have a good argument. I do sometimes, I guess there are times when I might actually er – let rip. But I usually have to be pushed pretty far before I'll argue. But if I do argue, people better run! [I laugh]

In other words, Peter is constructing himself in the above extract as someone who – although normally fairly placid – has an aggressive streak if he is provoked. It was as though men, by making such statements to me in the interview, were metaphorically 'roaring their masculine identity'. The impact of such comments on me as listener was to make me think of well-worn clichés such as 'his bark is worse than his bite' and I will come back to this point shortly. However, in the following section I want to underline the point that the presence of male threats can be debilitating for women.

The presence of threat

> It is possible to imagine that equally sophisticated Olympian and Chiltanic mystogogues met together in ecumenical consultations, discussing the merits of their respective universes *sine ira et studio* but, it is more likely that the issue was decided on the less rarefied level of military might. The historical outcome of each clash of gods was determined by those who wielded the better weapons rather than those who had the better arguments. The same, of course, may be said of intra-societal conflicts of this kind. He [*sic*] who has the bigger stick has the better chance of imposing his definitions of reality.
>
> (Berger and Luckmann 1966, p. 127)

Quite often, the comments men made concerning not being pushed around were corroborated by their wives in either joint or separate interviews. For example, Will Craven, when I asked if there was anything Karen ever tried to stop him doing, had this to say:

WILL: [pause] No, she's not – she's not one for telling me – she's never been one you know, for tellin me what to do or – or stop me – well, you know damn well it's no good tryin to stop me from doin it cause I'll do quite the opposite see…

Karen, in her separate interview, tells me:

KAREN: [pause] Um – well he either goes sort of one extreme to the other. He um – he's either very quiet – and sulky, or he's got a filthy temper. Cause he got a terrible temper you know if you – I mean I know now. I mean, I've known him long enough now to know that if he's in a p– in a temper – to keep quiet – cause if you try and say what's the matter or, have I done something or, anything along those lines, you know he'll – you know he can't control his temper it's just to – it's best to just be quiet until he calms down and he'll tell you then or [pause] you know…

Another similar discussion of male temper came from Heather Morris. When I arrived to do the second interviews with the Morrises it was rather embarrassing because Heather had not told Gerry that I was coming. She said she had forgotten. However, she also had this to say about how she managed to forget – in response to a question by me about whether she was very good at expressing herself to Gerry:

HEATHER: No, useless.

CAROLINE: Useless?

HEATHER: Yes. I, I tend not to have the right words at the right time. No – um, the night you rang up – I don't think he was home then – and um, he came in in a dreadful mood and I thought right, we won't say anything tonight, because, you know. Um – and of course it 'phew' gone, hadn't it. Um – but [pause] I you know, have to – tread carefully at times – oh dear but that wasn't the question.

In Heather's account, the challenge to equity – in the shape of shedding doubt on Gerry's egalitarian behaviour – is couched in self-blame but also suggests fear. For Gerry's part, in his separate interview, he makes the following comment:

GERRY: I think Heather um [pause] I think Heather will, very often won't say what she really feels for – for fear that she might upset me. Um, I don't feel I have quite the same um [pause] reserve – in that sense. Um – if I feel it's gotta be said, I'll say it and, um, huh – regret it afterwards more likely than not but um, so I think in that sense, um [pause] we're different.

Gerry Morris – in the joint interview with Heather – was keen to say that, although he had a temper, he would not want me to go away with the idea that he was violent. I think it is important to underline here that verbal violence can be extremely distressing and that, furthermore, a knowledge that your spouse has never actually hit you does not exclude the possibility of a 'first time'. The following extracts from interviews with the Prices illustrate these points.

The first extract is from the joint interview with the Prices, where I had just asked them how having children had affected their relationship:

RICHARD: [sigh of concentration] Well I wouldn't say, I mean, that some people say that children, if a marriage is on the rocks or, getting a bit like that, have a child and it brings you closer together. Now I would say that was an absolute load of rubbish [pause] because they can drive you right apart. I mean [pause] especially working shifts, it's not easy to [pause] you've gotta have a person you've gotta understand, well Margaret would have to understand me like, some days I gotta get up at 5 o'clock to get into work. There's nothing worse than having to be told by your wife in the middle of the night to get up and change a nappy or feed them when you're absolutely worn out and you've gotta be up at 5. Now, I didn't have that problem cause Margaret knows my shifts and [pause] I'm very fortunate that – um – she's very good like that. Now my poor old brother [pause] does a st– wasn't up at 5 but certainly very early and he would do everything.

Although, in the interview, we have been talking about the difficulties of having children, it is interesting to note here how Richard quickly talks about male sacrifice and the difficulty for him (see Chapter 3 on male sacrifice), whilst underplaying Margaret's tiredness and the stress of her own role. Furthermore, whether Margaret 'told' him to get up or got up herself, it is still her – in this scenario – that has the responsibility of listening and waking in the first place. However, the point I want to make here is that, once again, we see this 'I don't like being told' type of statement, i.e., 'There's nothing worse than having to be told by your wife in the middle of the night.' In other words, there is nothing worse than having your wife 'push you around'. Richard goes on to say in this extract that he was fortunate that Margaret did not do this.

Margaret, who in both interviews seemed a strong and determined sort of person, had this story to tell in her separate interview. She had been telling me that she and Richard had nearly split up recently. She said he had quite a nasty temper, and then told me this story:

MARGARET: I think actually it was just before you – you had come to see us, that we'd had um – hum – probably the biggest we'd ever had – and I told you about the phone being – off did I?

CAROLINE: No.

MARGARET: Um – this is going back about 18 months or so, and we'd had a very big row, and Richard's mother had phoned in the middle of it and I'd picked up the phone and was chatting 'normally'. Put the phone down – and somehow the line – between our two houses stayed open.

CAROLINE: Oh gosh!

MARGARET: Richard's Mum put the phone down – went and did some jobs, and about half an hour later picked up the phone and could hear – Richard screaming at me.

CAROLINE: Oh God!

MARGARET: Cause the line was still open. I mean it was totally fluke. But she could hear him. I sort of thought – gosh, who's that? – I could hear her shout Margaret! Margaret! Margaret! I could hear this shouting, and I went to the phone, she said, 'whatever's going on over there'. And – Richard's Mum and Dad, became involved at that – [not at the moment no – to child] – became involved because they heard – how Richard was reacting and they couldn't believe [pause] you know, the extent of his temper and – um – I

> almost, felt – Oh, thank goodness for that. Somebody else knows, and had heard.

Margaret Price was keen to tell me when I interviewed her that Richard had never been physically violent but that he was verbally aggressive. It is also interesting to note that Margaret talked about 'the problem' as being in some sense a joint one. In the following extract, when she first tells me about his temper, she uses 'we', and although this homogenising of 'the problem' means she has to shoulder some responsibility for it, it also seems to give her some control. Richard's temper has effectively been medicalised:

> MARGARET: Um, well Richard's got quite a nasty temper, which [children talking] and um – it all came to a head about three weeks ago and we'd had some guests here for a dinner party and um, to me R– Richard was just in a very [pause] strange mood. He was making [pause] comments, uum, toward me, which I found very upsetting. Um, I was asked to join in a quiz evening and, there was a – you know, a remark, for example: 'well if the questions are on *Coronation Street* and *Emmerdale Farm*, she'll be fine' and – just little things which really didn't help I mean, I'd slogged over – I'd slogged over the cooker all day and, you know, produced this meal I mean [pause]. Anyway, um [clearing throat] – we had a – a big – well we had a big row cause he does get a – a very nasty temper. And the following day, he continued and it, it – the children became involved and he got very, very angry, and very upset and – I knew he was gonna regret it and the more I kept on saying, 'you're gonna regret this' – the more wound up he was feeling. And he ended up shouting at the children and the children got very upset. And um, I said that I – I wasn't gonna put up with it [pause] um, once the children were starting to get involved. And he either had to sort himself out basically, or um – I didn't want to know. Which was very hard to say because I don't make threats, um – a – you know willy-nilly, because it just sort of devalues, devalues it. And um, I said, he either did something or we did something rather, um, or that would be it. And he was very upset and full of remorse and um – felt awful about it, but it's just something that takes over him. I mean he's never been violent, he's never ever – got even close to hitting any of us. It's just his – his – his [pause] hi– you know, his verbals really. Just terrible. Anyway, we went to see the doctor in the end, and um [clearing throat] he decided that, he needed some relaxation. So, um, we'll go and see the doctor now for half an hour appointments.

Reflecting back to the earlier section on men defining their masculinity by stepping outside of the couple, I talked about Richard Price in this connection and argued that men sometimes seemed to step outside of a notion of partnership because they had difficulty controlling the marital agenda. During my interviews with Richard and Margaret, Margaret continually made use of the relational 'we', as in the above extract, and it was clear that she had been highly instrumental in organising the visit to the doctor. Richard could be construed as in some senses losing control through Margaret's action. Parallels here can therefore be drawn with earlier examples of the use of 'we' by men as a way of controlling the marital agenda. However, the difference between Margaret's construction of 'we' and, for example, Gordon Evans' construction is that the latter serves to conceal his selfish behaviour in making sure that his wife had to care for her mother rather than allow her mother to go into a home. As far as Margaret's use of 'we' is concerned, although this gives her some circumscribed control, such a construction works to protect Richard from blame for his violent behaviour and construe Margaret as partly responsible. Furthermore, Margaret still has to live with a constant presence of threat, whether of verbal or physical violence.

The final case I want to examine briefly in this section is that of Tim and Marion Hughes. I have said very little about this couple to date, except that Tim was unemployed at the time of both interviews and Marion appeared to have sole responsibility for housework and child-care. In the original joint interview with the Hugheses, Marion had this to say at one point (she had just said that she tends to panic with the youngest child):

MARION: Whereas he's [Tim] placid and calm you know.
CAROLINE: Yeah.
MARION: [laughing] Sometimes [pause] But he can be a bit of a swine [I laugh awkwardly].
TIM: Carry on! [she laughs] I'm placid today [he laughs – which is unusual in the interview].
MARION: Yeah, well you could be a right – pain in the arse tomorrow.

Eighteen months later, when I interviewed the spouses separately, Tim's behaviour seemed particularly strange. He used the first part of his separate interview to shout through to the kitchen abusive remarks meant for Marion's ears. However, Marion soon left the house and I decided to terminate the interview at this point because I felt 'uneasy'. The best way to convey a flavour of my 'uneasy feeling' in this interview is to transcribe the following short extract from my conversation with Tim (we had been talking about Tim's unemployment and the problems of having no money):

CAROLINE: Yeah. It's obviously a strain and a worry and it's obviously a strain and a worry for Marion as well isn't it?
TIM: Is it?
CAROLINE: Yeah.
TIM: Didn't know women had feelings.
CAROLINE: [slight murmured laugh]
TIM: Have they?

CAROLINE: [I nod.]
TIM: Oh.

Coupled with my recollection of Tim's comment in the first interview with the couple, where he had talked about 'scheming women – they're all scheming', I started to feel extremely uncomfortable about Tim's attitude towards women.

'Woman hate' and male insecurity

In his book, *Masculinity and Power*, Brittan (1989) argued that men as a group do not find pornography objectionable because men as a group do not treat women as respect-worthy. Tim Hughes, in the example given above, was clearly not treating me as respect-worthy and neither did he treat his wife as such during my interviews with the couple. Other examples I have discussed in the chapter also indicated this lack of respectful behaviour on the part of husbands. In the same way, some of the men I interviewed told me, often in front of their wives, about 'prejudiced attitudes' that still existed – for example, in relation to women's ability in the workplace – and which they themselves shared. Two such examples of this I have already related when I talked about Nick Freeman and Malcolm Anderson 'stepping into intergroup mode' at the beginning of this chapter. The following is another such example from a separate interview with Mike Walters:

MIKE: I think um, if you have to, contact a firm, for whatever reason, and the person you're talking to is a woman, if she is of the [pause] same rank, as the bloke you've been talking to, in the same job, you don't feel, as if you're talking to the right person. You're talking to a woman. It's just one of those things that still carries on, you don't think they know enough about it.
CAROLINE: Right, yeah.
MIKE: They probably do. They may even be better at the job than the equivalent bloke but er, on the whole you don't – feel that you're getting satisfaction.
CAROLINE: So you think attitudes are still…
MIKE: Yeah, still with the underdog being a woman.

There are three points I want to make about the above statement. First, Mike, by talking in terms of 'the problem' being 'just one of those things that still carries on', is effectively dislocating himself from 'the problem', and in the same way, he succeeds in doing this by talking in the general form of 'you'. By using such conversation devices, he is able to convey his own 'view' on the state of affairs whilst distancing himself from responsibility for the statement. The second point I want to make is that Mike, in suggesting that women sometimes seem to be insufficiently competent, is effectively not only absolving men from blame for the situation, but also placing the onus on women to 'work even harder' to engender men's confidence. All men can do, in this scenario, is to wait patiently and see whether women develop sufficiently to be trusted. The third point I want to make here is to express surprise that Mike felt able to make such a comment in the first place, whether couched in terms of the general form of 'you' or not. Given that he knew I was a woman, and given that he knew I was interviewing him as part of my job, his comment could be seen as rude.

In fact, an analysis of my data revealed that 'rude' comments from the men to me as well as to their wives were quite common. However, I had to come away from the face-to-face interview situation to see this. At the time, I realise now, I made 'allowances' for such comments and, in a sense, barely heard them. This was partly because they were all too familiar to me: as a woman, there is almost an immunity to the registering of such comments, so commonly are they heard. However, I think it was also partly because, at the time of the interviews, I felt sorry for some of the men I spoke to, particularly when they said things that led me to feel they were 'having an identity crisis'. In order to explain what I mean here, I want to return to my data.

It is interesting to note that while most of the men implicitly, and sometimes explicitly, located the 'problem' of gender inequality in women, the nearest any of the women came in my study group to blaming men for such inequality was when Janet Campbell talked about issues such as child abuse. I asked Janet how she felt about men in general and she had this to say:

JANET: Oh God. Um [pause] well again I mean that is terribly difficult, because, I mean we – we – the people we mix with, um [pause] you know, then those men – are fine – generally. Um – but then I'm very aware that there's this – other – [laughing] group of men – and having, I mean, um – like last week – last week or the week before I was in court observing, and it was a rape case, and the week before I was in a court, and it was um – it was um [pause] indecent assault on a 5-year-old little girl, and that tends to, you know, colour – colour your judgement really on men – um – because [pause] you know, I – I realise that the people we mix with are – probably [pause] a minority. That there's this – I mean I know a lot of women who – who would actually say that they hate men – generally would hate – well you know – haven't got much time for, most men. And I can understand, I mean I'm beginning to understand that point of view, how people feel – um – if they've experienced a bad time. Um [pause] I think the majority of them are – still [pause] well I think probably what it is is er – tends to be an insecurity that they have and that's why they – treat women – the way they do, um, or talk of women in the way they do.

CAROLINE: What – an insecurity?

JANET: That they have.

CAROLINE: That they're insecure in what way?

JANET: Um [pause] well just that they [pause] well I – I mean – their role, what – what a lot of men – what they believe their role is is to be. Tough and um – capable. Um – and [pause] I mean there's, you know, very few men – are

> like that. Um – but they're expected – they're you know, there are expectations for them to be like that. And – and so [pause] I mean I think that makes them – vulnerable but they're not able to cope with that vulnerability. Whereas women don't tend to get that – pushed upon them. Um – and therefore are able to show their – vulnerabilities, you know.

To come back to the point I made above, that I often felt sorry for the men I interviewed, particularly if I felt they were having an 'identity crisis', my sentiments are reflected in Janet's statement above. There are three points I want to make here. First, I want to underline the now familiar message in this book that this type of account of men's behaviour effectively absolves men from responsibility for their behaviour. As such, it bears a striking resemblance to most of the contemporary sex role development and identity literature (see Brittan 1989 for a review in relation to masculinity). Second, the missing link in Janet's statement, and in my own perception of my conversations with some of the men in my interview, is that being masculine – or 'doing masculinity' – in the way I have described it in this chapter – was the same thing as 'doing oppression'. Mike Walters' comment to me above formed part of my experience of oppression, and I have already attempted to demonstrate in this chapter the ways in which other men I interviewed constructed their wives' experience of oppression in part through what they said. Given this, we need to take Janet's assertion above that 'what a lot of men – believe their role is, is to be tough and capable' and add 'as measured by how effectively they can mark the status distance between self and woman, or self and wife, or, in other words, how effectively they can oppress women'. The crudest form of this construction in my interviews was in the open verbal aggression meted out to his wife and to 'women in general' – including me – by Tim Hughes.

The third point I want to make concerning Janet's statement, and my own feelings of sympathy towards men who seemed to be struggling to define their masculinity, is that this empathic stance towards male oppression takes attention away from women's suffering. I suggest that the issue of male insecurity and vulnerability has served as a smoke screen, blocking any attention to something that my data analysis highlighted as a major issue for the women in my study group – that of women's insecurity. In the following chapter, I want to turn to this issue and, in so doing, move to discuss an aspect of marriage that I have not as yet mentioned – namely, the subject of love and affection in marriage.

6

THE WASTELAND AT THE CROSSROADS OF A MARRIAGE

A husband's construction of a wife's insecurity

In focusing throughout this book so far on interview talk as active and constructive and identity as an 'accomplishment' or 'work' that people engage in (West and Zimmerman 1991), I have simultaneously been working from the perspective that there is more to life than text. As I said in Chapter 1, although there will never be a way to view reality that is stripped of human meaning, that doesn't mean no reality exists. Neither does it imply that we should stop trying to make meaning about the nature of that reality. Throughout this book so far I have been using an analysis of my understanding of people's talk and action in the interviews to try to shed light on how I think they might have been feeling *during* but also, *before* or *after* the interview, in relation to their married lives together. I have also, in places, been implicitly speculating on how people might have been likely to be *behaving* in various aspects of their married lives outside of the interview. For example, I have argued there was considerable evidence from listening to couples talking about their lives that the women in my study group were still predominantly responsible for housework and child-care.

In this chapter, in similar vein to the biographies of Chapter 2, I want to venture still further outside of an analysis of the 'dynamics of the moment' and use interview accounts to explore evidence of husbands' separation behaviour in marriage and the likely emotional consequences of this separation behaviour for wives. This, then, is the final leg of my investigation of the interrelations between marital identity, gender power relations and human emotional experience. My starting point for the final leg is the topic of love and affection in a marital relationship.

Love and affection in marriage

Listening to people's stories about their relationships, and watching couples interacting with each other in interviews, there was evidence of the majority (although not all) of the people in my study having strong emotional bonds with, and feelings of affection for, their partners. One of the most telling signs of the power of emotional bonds in the marriages I studied came from comments that reflected a fear of being left. This can be seen, for example, in the following two extracts from women in their separate interviews. The first is with Emma Scott:

CAROLINE: Do you ever feel, um, in any way that Tom is part of you?
EMMA: [pause] Oh yes, yes. Very much so. I mean I – I can't imagine life without – without him really at all, I mean I've tried to. I – emotionally I'm extremely – dependent on him. Extremely dependent on him and I – I couldn't cope at all, emotionally. If he suddenly walked out the door I mean I – I'd, become a jelly fish or something. I mean I – [pause] at least I think that's what'd happen [both laugh a bit].

In the same way, Karen Craven, in her separate interview, has this to say when I ask if she feels that Will is at all part of her:

KAREN: Yes I do. Yeah. Yeah. You know, you t– try and think of um – life without them. You know, it – I know it's morbid things to think about but I mean, these things happen. It's funny, whenever I go to a funeral – I know it's morbid! [laughing a bit] – don't go to many but you know you sort of stand there an you think, you know, God what would I do if anything ever happened to you? You know an [pause] it's like a great chunk – being taken out of me life, you know cause – however hard you try not to be dependent but you know, emotionally as well you know you sort of – you don't appreciate each other until you haven't – you've got – you know, got each other I don't think. I think you do yeah.

The expression of emotional dependence and fear of what would happen to self without the partner seemed as real to some of the men in my study as to the women. Will Craven, for example, talked about how he missed Karen when she was away for a few days in hospital with their child, and Brian Thompson had this to say:

CAROLINE: How do you think friends or family might sort of see your marriage, looking in on it?
BRIAN: Pretty – happy I should think. In fact somebody in work who doesn't know Cathy sort of – um – who I haven't known very long, she says you seem really happy with your wife, cause you know we're always talking about – things in work, and she says – oh it's nice to see – cause we got married so young. We were talking about that and she said, well, you always seem so ha– you know, quite happy, you don't seem to have anything – I mean I call her 'the dragon' but everyone does. [I laugh awkwardly]. That's a term of endearment.
[and then, a few mintues later:]
CAROLINE: Do you ever feel that Cathy's a part of you in any way?

BRIAN: Yeah, I think so – yeah. Er [pause] I don't know what I'd do without her to be honest.
CAROLINE: Right. Ah [as in that's nice].
BRIAN: But don't tell her that [we both laugh].

In this extract then, despite Brian's disrespectful use of the term 'the dragon' to describe his wife, he suggests that he would actually be lost without her and I felt convinced, having interviewed him, that this would indeed be the case.

In fact, it is interesting to note here that, while I have talked in the last chapter about the pervasive tendency for men to step outside of the notion of partnership and define the masculine 'I', some of these self-same men talked elsewhere in the interviews about their emotional bonds with their wives. For example, Mike Walters had this to say in his joint interview when I asked if either of them could describe what love meant to them:

MIKE: S'pose it's the sort of feeling that you're better off together than – apart. You would miss each other, so – there's something more than [pause] like a friend, you can say 'cheerio' and – and go off but er – you feel lost without the other half.
[exclamation from Liz and she and I laugh]
MIKE: And you – do things together.

This notion of being part of a relational whole seems particularly odd, given some of Mike's comments quoted in Chapter 4, which I argued had the effect of undermining his wife's construction of relational identity. It is also interesting to note here that Liz seems surprised and pleased by Mike's remark, as though it is unusual. In fact, although such comments from the men were not that unusual in the interviews, when they occurred they were invariably greeted with expressions of welcoming surprise from the women. It is also worth noting that Brian said 'but don't tell her' when he told me that he'd be lost without Cathy. Furthermore, my reaction to his comment – 'Ah' as in, 'that's nice' – implies that I also experienced the same feeling of surprise that Brian had made such an admission.

I would suggest that the picture that I am painting so far about statements of affection and love has a common currency. Popular magazines – particularly the 'problem pages' – attest to men's reticence at talking about their feelings. Television and radio programmes, as well as romantic novels, also construct this kind of image. A popular theme in both the media and in psychological approaches to the emotional aspects of relationships seems to be: it isn't that men don't have feelings, or don't care for their loved ones, they just can't show it very well, or, it isn't very masculine to show it.

The idea in such analysis is that men find it very painful to express emotion, perhaps even because they are physiologically not very well prepared to cope with intense feelings (Gottman and Levenson 1986). For writers such as Gottman and Levenson, the problem is often compounded by women demanding shows of affection – which tend to make men even more reticent than they were to start with. Such theories have popular resonance and are common in analyses of communication breakdown in marriage. I want to argue in the rest of this chapter that, as I have started to indicate above, there was evidence that several of the men in my sample probably did have strong feelings for their wives. There is also considerable evidence that – not just in the interview situation – they were not very forthcoming in showing their feelings. In trying to make sense of this reticence, however, I will be arguing that we need to focus on gender power relations.

Men's separation behaviour

One of the most striking features across the whole of my interview data, was that, despite claims of partnership and closeness from quite a few of the men, nearly every woman in my study talked at some stage about ways in which their husband appeared to distance himself from her in some way or another. Most of the women I interviewed were outgoing, active people who had friends of their own outside of their relationship (usually from child-care contacts during the day) and some of the women in my study also had evening commitments – often to do with their children. However, descriptions of separation behaviour by husbands were often tinged with a feeling of sadness. For example, Marion Hughes, in her separate interview with me – at which time her marriage was clearly in difficulties – had this to say:

MARION: I, well, I always fancy that when you're married together, you do things together, you know, you don't sort of – you go one way and he go the other, you – you do it together. But um, it's not always been like that – with us, you know.

In the original joint interview, the couple have this exchange:

TIM: I prefer, my own company. Cause I used to, when we first got married I used to disappear, for half a day, I/

MARION: And I could– I couldn't the– you know. I thought, well, you know, he wanted to get married and, he wanted to marry me, and I thought well, why does he keep going off on his own, you know?

The main ways men appeared to cut themselves off from their wives – and often children – I was told, were by: watching television, dropping off to sleep in the chair in front of the television, not talking enough, refusing to go out with wife, going out without wife, and doing too much overtime. Such patterns of behaviour by men were reported as an issue with most of the women I interviewed and none of the men I interviewed challenged such accounts. The following gives a flavour of what I have termed 'separation behaviour':

Karen Craven told me that Will dropped off to sleep in the chair most nights at about 7 o'clock and it was often difficult to get him to talk to her. She sometimes had to choose her moment to talk. She also found it hard to persuade Will to go out with her.

Joan Docherty told me that Peter generally dropped off to sleep in front of the television at weekends and often would not really engage in conversation with her.

Heather Morris told me that Gerry came in at night and watched television until 'the dot came up' on the screen, and then went to bed and picked up his book. She also told me that she had to 'tread carefully' sometimes and pick her moment for talking to him about various issues. Furthermore, if Heather and Gerry went out socially, Heather explained that it would have to be by his instigation because he wouldn't like it if she made the arrangements. As he rarely made arrangements to go out, they rarely went out. Heather told me she was unsure what men wanted out of marriage.

Liz Walters told me that she and Mike rarely talked about anything much, and that he generally went out on his own. She also told me that he sometimes worked overtime until the early hours of the morning. Such a picture stands in stark contrast to Mike's comment, transcribed earlier, in which he talks about love in terms of doing things together.

Cathy Thompson told me that ever since they had been married Brian had spent most of his spare time going out 'with his mates' and playing sport. He never came home when he said he was going to and this used to upset her in the early years of their marriage. She wondered how he could love her if he didn't want to be with her. However, she had become more resigned to this behaviour of late, although she couldn't really understand what men wanted out of marriage.

Emma Scott told me that Tom watched a lot of television and Tom told me that Emma sometimes got cross because he didn't talk to her enough. The couple also talked about Tom's dislike of socialising and how this was an issue between them – for example, when Tom failed to accompany Emma to a social event with her work colleages. Emma suggested that some of her work colleagues might think Tom was a 'myth'.

Sarah Anderson told me that Malcolm watched too much television, and she was also clearly unhappy about the amount of time Malcolm spent away from the house on overtime at work, commenting at various intervals throughout interviews about the fact that he was 'hardly ever there'.

Wendy Spencer told me that Neil was always watching television and that it was difficult to find the chance to talk to him. He wouldn't go out with her, and spent most of his time, when not watching television, at his allotment.

Janet Campbell's husband Simon told me that television was sometimes an issue because Janet felt it 'prevented a normal discourse' between them. Janet told me that Simon frequently 'dropped off' in front of the television and was asleep for the whole evening and then went to bed. She also told me that it was difficult to get him to talk about some things.

Margaret and Richard Price argued in front of me about Richard's 'desire to go out on his own', Richard telling us both that if he was 'allowed out' more then he would feel more inclined to do home maintenance chores.

Carol Matthews told me that Tony didn't like going out much and, as she did, she generally had to go out on her own.

Sally Freeman told me in their interviews that the couple rarely talked about anything much, and Nick commented that this used to worry Sally but he felt that she was used to it now.

Marion Hughes, by the time of my second interview, had clearly given up much hope of a close and sharing relationship with Tim, as the earlier extract illustrates.

Of the four couples who did *not* discuss the above kind of behaviour as being an issue in their marriage, I used data from two of the couples, the Hendersons and the Evanses in Chapter 5. I argued there that Patrick Henderson and Gordon Evans were able to use relational identification as a vehicle for constructing hierarchical gender difference within their marriage. Perhaps, therefore, they did not 'need' physically to cut themselves off from their wives in this kind of way in order to mark out a status difference between self and wife. With the third couple, the Wrights, Amanda nevertheless told me that she had felt depressed on and off since she got married, initially because she felt lonely and isolated. With the onset of her disability Jim had to help Amanda with some of the child-care duties and perhaps this had alleviated feelings of isolation – although not of depression. With the fourth couple not mentioned so far, Joanna and Bernard Hardy in some senses appeared to have a qualitatively different relationship from the other people in my study and I will briefly turn to focus on the Hardys here.

The Hardys' relationship appeared to be qualitatively different from the relationships of the other couples in my study because, for the Hardys, gender inequality was not a secret or something that should be 'swept under the carpet'. Although Joanna prefaced her comments with the disclaimer 'I'm not a feminist but…' (see Griffin 1989 for further discussion of this type of disclaimer) she was outspoken in her beliefs about women's oppression, talking about ways in which she felt women could lose their identity through the traditional roles and the restricted choices they face. Joanna and Bernard were also open in discussing disagreements that they have about division of labour. In fact, Bernard was the only man I interviewed to show any sign of guilt on the subject of women's oppression, in the sense of offering to take some responsibility for trying to change things through 'giving up' some of his socially constructed privilege. In the following extract, the couple have been discussing societal pressures to conform:

BERNARD: Let me, quote you a simple example [pause] of something which could put pressure on. [pause] Um [pause] end of – end of the working day, my boss comes along and says, do you wanna come over the pub for a pint. Now last night I actually did it, and I did it – one of the reasons I did it was cause I've said no, several times in the past. I don't particularly like doing that, but I don't particularly dislike doing it either. But I know that – if I did it regularly, it is a bit of an imposition on Joanna. You know. Why should I have the pleasure/

JOANNA: Well, [I'd be totally pissed off if you did that, cause it means the
BERNARD: [relaxing in the pub.
JOANNA: end of the day is a very busy [time of the day.
BERNARD: [Right. But that is – it is a gender-related thing because it tends to be things do/
JOANNA: Yes it's something that males take for granted.
BERNARD: Yeah.
JOANNA: I s'pose other males would put you down for certain/
BERNARD: Exactly! now that's the thing. Now, there are a couple of classic/
JOANNA: Going home to the good little wife.
BERNARD: occasions and two of the directors [pause] who, they're always going on about, this sort of – it's the sort of – getting up the pub, getting away from 'the dragon' thing – which – I mean just appalls me. Why be married if you're trying to get away from somebody all the time, but a lot of people do it.

In the above extract, Joanna has raised the issue of the practical consequences, in terms of workload, of a man going to the pub in the evening, and Bernard's comment reflects the emotional aspects of such separation. In making this comment, I believe he reflected a question that some of the other women in my study had been grappling with themselves. In the following three sections, I want to turn to discuss in more detail the practical and emotional consequences of men's separation behaviour.

Workload and separation

Evidence of the practical benefits for men of separating from their wives – whether by 'losing themselves in the television', dropping off to sleep or going out to the pub – came in the form of the difficulties this kind of behaviour caused in relation to child-care and domestic labour. For example, one of Joan Docherty's recurring grievances was that Peter would go into the lounge after lunch at the weekend, switch on the television and watch it for the whole afternoon – or drop off to sleep in front of it. This meant, not only that he did not play with the children or take them out, but also that he did not hear the children if they started to have a fight with each other or wanted something etc. In other words, he took no responsibility for caring for the children at the weekends. In the same way, Cathy Thompson had this to say about Sundays in her household:

CAROLINE: What time do you get together, as a family if you like? Do you get any time together, the two of you/
CATHY: Sunday afternoons [in a gloomy tone].
CAROLINE: Right. What's that like? Is that – difficult, or boring or nice or?
CATHY: It's quite difficult actually cause he falls asleep, and the children have usually been in all day and then they're all bored and they wanna go out and [pause]
CAROLINE: Dunno what to do with them?
CATHY: No [pause] I don't like Sundays very much.

In the same way, if men went out on their own or worked a lot of overtime, this meant that home maintenance was not carried out or husbands were able to avoid domestic labour. Decisions about how much overtime to work did not seem to have been jointly negotiated by the couples. With Sarah Anderson, for example, she clearly felt that Malcolm worked too much overtime and furthermore, Malcolm talked at various points in their second interview about how much he enjoyed his work. The implication from some of Sarah's comments was that she would have liked him to do less overtime and more around the house, and that overtime for Malcolm was in some sense an escape from his home responsibilities. In the same way, Cathy Thompson pointed out that, because Brian played a lot of sport, she did not get much of a break from child-care in the early evenings, and she herself worked two nights a week. Furthermore, her work, coupled with his social life, meant that she rarely saw him to talk to, and it is to the issue of communication that I will turn next.

Separation, communication and control

I have pointed out above that lack of communication between partners was a constant grievance amongst the women in my study. Given the economic dependence of most of the women on their husbands, verbal communication was vital in order to (1) find out what was happening in the husband's sphere of work and (2) have some input into decisions her husband might make that could affect their future. For example, Janet Campbell's husband ran his own business, and he employed a staff of twenty-six people. The future of Simon's business was clearly as much Janet's concern as his, for she had no independent means of her own and the couple had two children for whom Janet had major responsibility. However, both Janet and Simon indicated that he was often reticent about the business. Simon, in his separate interview, said he tended to 'totally divorce the family from work', and that he preferred things this way, although Janet's account was slightly different:

JANET: The classic thing is that he'll come home, and it'll be – doom and gloom, you know, and – and if [firm] is still going in January I'll be surprised, bla-di-bla, you see, and then I spend the next two days – kind of worrying about it.

She goes on to say that, in the meantime, Simon has 'had his moan' about it and he seems to be alright. However, to find out more, Janet has to 'niggle and badger' – in her words – to get things out of him.

I would suggest here that Simon, in keeping discussions on the business to a minimum, was able to have the best of both worlds. He could 'have his moan' when he came home and therefore ease the burden of the worry by sharing this with his wife. However, he then closed off discussion on the topic in order that he could keep control of the future course of events. It is worth noting here that Janet complained at one or two points in the interview that Simon never took her advice on anything. Other women in my study made similar comments and furthermore, as I have pointed out above, one or two of the women commented that they had to 'pick their moment' before talking about certain topics.

In this connection, it is important to note that the meaning ascribed to Simon's unwillingness to discuss the business was couched in the language of determinism in the interviews with Janet and Simon. Both spouses described Janet as 'a worrier' to me, thereby effectively locating the problem within her. Simon at no time acknowledged to me that in 'shutting her out' from discussions about the business, he might be giving Janet something to worry about. In other words, Simon was able to develop a determinist argument to 'explain' Janet's experience of anxiety over the business, and the discourse of biological determinism protected Simon from having the legitimacy of his own behaviour questioned.

However, I would emphasise here that Janet clearly pushed Simon to discuss the business, and her comment that he never took her advice on anything indicated that she was keen to give such advice. Verbal exchange could well prove a threat to established explanations of events and (as I touched on in Chapter 5) I would suggest here that, in order to protect the status quo, it might sometimes be easier for husbands not to talk. Silence can be a powerful weapon.

Isolation

The full impact of men's separation behaviour for women was, I believe, to create a sense of isolation – particularly for women who had been trapped in the house all day with young children and no adult company. Karen Craven, for example, had this to say concerning her husband's tendency to drop off to sleep in the chair every night, and it is worth mentioning here that Karen's hours of work are just as long as Will's:

KAREN: I think, you know, a lot of – well it's not problems but, you know, every, every relationship has ups and downs doesn't it but – I think a lot of it is due to just sort of – well Will's tired, you know, and he's gotta get up at half past five every morning. Well [pause] he's usually gone to sleep half past seven at night you know, well I mean – it's understandable isn't it really but sometimes it makes me cross an I'm sort of sat there an I think well you know, I just be sat on me own really – than just sat here with a body [laughing a bit] – cause that's all it is.

In the following extract, from my conversation with Wendy Spencer following Neil's departure from the house, Wendy talks about her husband's television-watching behaviour, and this extract seems to capture some of the loneliness that Wendy appeared to be feeling:

CAROLINE: Saying about Neil finding it hard, sort of not really wanting to talk about this [marriage], do you think it's harder for men in general, to talk about things like this or – is it just [pause] a bit?

WENDY: Well I don't know. Depends on your personality dunn't it. Cause I mean my brother he's in Australia he's, [pause] oh he's, he's very open and he's very [pause] he's completely different – he's the opposite to Neil, he comes home and looks after the kids and things and the nappies and – and all these kind of things and he does [pause] it just depends on how you are. And I mean, he does – he's, his relationship, the way he behaves is very, very much like his father.

CAROLINE: Um – what Neil you mean?

WENDY: Yeah. Neil's father went to work, and left his wife home to do the housework

CAROLINE: Mm.

WENDY: and then came home and watched the television.

CAROLINE: Yeah.

WENDY: And this is what Neil is doing [both laugh]. Only he, he didn't like to admit it [more laughs].

CAROLINE: Do you row about that or?

WENDY: No I don't.

CAROLINE: You don't.

WENDY: I do, I do – I moan actually. And say, for goodness sake what – or you know moan about the tele or something – rather than saying point blank look you ah – but then then I don't think it – I should say to him look you should not watch the telvision. Because as he's already said, he doesn't do anything else – in the winter. He does in the summer.

CAROLINE: Do you think you're more – outgoing than he is/

WENDY: Much.

CAROLINE: Yeah, right [pause].

WENDY: And that's the reason why I didn't answer the thing about the friends because – Neil's not a sociable person. And that's the reason why I told you you won't get much out of him [laughing].

CAROLINE: Do you think it's quite difficult to do a joint interview like this, I mean, I've never asked anybody that so far with doing the interviews but [pause] er is it easier to talk on your own, do you think, with people or?

WENDY: No – it's easier to be asked questions.

CAROLINE: What, on [your own or together?

WENDY: [No, no it's nice to be able to talk together because then I can listen, because he doesn't – say a lot. He's a very quiet person – and probably some things he said tonight he would never have said.

CAROLINE: Yeah.

WENDY: So I quite like to listen.

CAROLINE: Cause he did say quite a few things tonight/

WENDY: He did.

CAROLINE: Didn't he yeah, yeah.

WENDY: But I mean he, he is a loner. He goes [pause] he's an only child [pause] he's never had a, a – what do you call them – sibling? – to play with, and er [pause] at work he, he, at dinner time he goes for a walk around the area, on his own usually. So he, he spends a lot of time on his own.

CAROLINE: Yeah [pause].

WENDY: And he had got, he does think that – his – role in life is to provide the money and the [pause] security in the house.

CAROLINE: Yeah – he's got quite a traditional attitude?

WENDY: And he gets up early and goes to work and comes home tired [pause] and likes his tea [laughing slightly] when he gets home, and then he, he feels that he's [pause] entitled to relax in the evenings. And he does relax by watching television.

CAROLINE: Yeah, right. And what would you, would you rather do something else in the evenings or?

WENDY: [pause] Well I do do something else. I'm not, I don't usually sit and watch [tele.

CAROLINE: [Oh I see, yeah.

WENDY: I just usually fiddle.

CAROLINE: Yeah, I do that actually [both laugh].

WENDY: [I never watch, I never watch a programme because

CAROLINE: [or walk around and do things.

WENDY: I can't concentrate when everyone's there. So I don't watch – unless it's something I really like and there are a few programmes…

[…]

CAROLINE: Does Neil watch *EastEnders*?

WENDY: He does watch it. He says he doesn't like it but, but you see he's a compulsive television watcher [laughing] and he'll watch anything. We were having lunch today – just came home from the interview [he had been for a job interview] and I wanted to hear all about it, and he switched the television on and watched the children's programmes! Because he just doesn't like er

CAROLINE: Talking?

WENDY: No, He doesn't like talking very much.

[...]

WENDY: And I have tried – to get everybody to sit at the table to eat tea [pause] and switch the television off – but that doesn't work because it's always – *Grange Hill* or something that they've been following, and they want to watch the next episode, or then it's the news, and they don't, they want to see – mind you I don't know why you want to watch the news at 6 o'clock when it's on again at 9 o'clock but [laughing] and there's always something or other. I mean, if I've made a roast dinner or something special they will all sit at the table, and stay there, but it's – as soon as the tea's put on the table – and it's – 'Oh please can I go and watch that other thing' [laughing] after all your efforts they sort of bring their plates down [laughing] and I always sit at the table so I'm left on my own.

In the above extract, Wendy mentions Neil's television-watching behaviour on various occasions. She also mentions that he has been for a job interview that day, but came home and watched children's television rather than talking to her about the interview. As with Simon Campbell, discussed above, I suggest that such separation behaviour would serve to protect Neil from too much influence by Wendy. Wendy was clearly the more eloquent of the two, and he may well have been unable to win an argument with her, unless he resorted to verbal aggression – which, as Wendy intimated in the joint interview, he was sometimes inclined to do.

I felt sad after I had interviewed Wendy and concerned that, whereas with most of the women the interviews seemed to have given them a welcome chance to talk about such issues, for Wendy the discussion seemed to make her miserable. I have already mentioned that most of the women I interviewed were outgoing, active people. Wendy had made her own day-time friends during her years of caregiving, and although the force of her comments about Neil's television watching, not talking and generally being unresponsive, indicated that this was a constant worry for her, I believe she probably coped with day-to-day life by pushing such issues to the back of her mind. The interview brought such issues to the fore and her apparent unhappiness was clearly compounded by Neil's behaviour in the joint interview, where he was often monosyllabic and bordered on the rude. It is interesting to note in the above extract that after she tells me that she 'quite likes to listen' to what he has to say – because he normally doesn't talk very much – I say, 'cause he did say quite a few things tonight'. I made this comment because I wanted to give Wendy reassurance concerning Neil's feelings for her. At the conclusion of our discussion she commented that talking about these topics:

WENDY: Makes you think doesn't it. Makes you think about things that you haven't probably thought about for a long time.

I left Wendy's house worrying that Wendy had begun to dwell on whether or not Neil loved her. I decided not to ask the couple if I could interview them again, partly because, as I said in Chapter 5, I had separate data from my discussion alone with Wendy and I was less than keen to interview Neil alone. Partly, however, I decided not to go back to the couple because I did not want to precipitate any more introspection for Wendy around the status of her relationship. I believe Wendy was already feeling insecure, and I did not want to make her feel worse.

Women's insecurity

There was evidence from my interviews that about three-quarters of the women I interviewed experienced feelings of insecurity as, for example, the following extract from my separate interview with Tom Scott suggests. I have just asked Tom if he ever worries about Emma's feelings for him, and he says no. I then ask if he thinks she ever worries about his feelings for her and he says:

TOM: [pause] Sometimes, I think she does, yeah. If we've had a litt– argument or something. You know, perhaps she thinks well 'I've gone off her' or something like that. But it's – it's just something that, you know, crops up, flares up and then just – diminishes then. You know. Cause you know, obviously we have arguments and things like that [details of arguments].

CAROLINE: Why do you think there's that difference, in her feeling that – you know – sometimes?

TOM: I dunno. I don't think it's – er insecurity or anything but, um [longish pause] I'm just wondering, do – do women think along those lines? You know, sort of

CAROLINE: Yeah [as in, 'I see what you mean'].

TOM: [pause] more so than men maybe. I don't know, I don't – wouldn't like to say but I – I do sometimes think that Emma well thinks oh – perhaps I've gone off her or something. You know. If we have a little argument, or, something.

CAROLINE: Yeah – certainly [pause] it sort of rings a bell as a kind of a – gender issue.

TOM: Yeah, mm.

In the above conversation with Tom I do not directly challenge his analysis, and I will return to this issue later. However, the point I want to make here is that he is suggesting that Emma's 'worry' about his feelings might be something to do with women; i.e. once again the problem has been located in the disposition of the woman. However, although Emma's account concurs with the idea that she sometimes feels a bit insecure about Tom's feelings for her, I would argue that her 'worry' could be related in large measure to the fact that Tom sometimes engaged in the separation behaviour discussed above. For example, they both told me that she sometimes found it hard to get him to communicate with her, and he often refused to accompany her to social functions. She commented that some of her friends must think that Tom was a 'myth', and I believe Emma felt insecure because Tom's behaviour threatened the solidarity of the couple and made her wonder why he was sometimes so withdrawn.

In fact, I have already mentioned above that some of the women made comments along the lines of Bernard Hardy's dialogue transcribed earlier. Namely, if someone loves you, why do they not want to spend any time with you or talk to you? In the next section of this chapter, I want to develop this argument and attempt to demonstrate that, not only was husbands' separation behaviour related to feelings of insecurity in wives, but also that some of the men I interviewed seemed unashamedly to try to foster such feelings of insecurity. At this point, I would like to reflect on an extract from Brian Thompson's interview reproduced earlier. Brian told me that he would be lost without Cathy. But he also laughed and said to me – 'but don't tell her'. From my discussion with Cathy it was apparent that such information from Brian would have been welcome. Then why had he not made a habit of giving her this reassurance, and why did he ask me not to tell her? The question I would like to raise here is 'since when has it been socially acceptable to try to make someone feel insecure?'

Constructing women's insecurity

One of the questions that I asked people in separate interviews was whether they thought they cared enough for their spouse, and whether they thought their spouse cared enough for them (unless I felt that this would be a completely inappropriate thing to ask, for example, where someone had just told me they were worried about such issues, or seemed upset). A common pattern in this connection was for men to say that they really did care enough about their wives but that they probably didn't show it; this view was usually endorsed by their wives. Some of the men referred to what they described as their wife's insecurity and suggested that perhaps they could do more to put her mind at rest sometimes 'only…'. It was this 'only…' that I found really quite strange. In the same way that Brian Thompson had said 'don't tell her' that he would be lost without her, other men in the sample didn't seem to feel that there was a real problem telling me that they were less than forthcoming in their shows of affection towards their wives. However, these same men were generally quick to say that their wives gave them all the affection they wanted.

The point here, I would argue, was that implying that they were a bit thoughtless in this respect was one of the ways in which men appeared to define a sense of masculine self. In this way, it often appeared to be more socially acceptable for a man to play down any caring behaviour than to play down a sense of neglect. For example, in Mike Walters' separate interview with me he has this to say:

MIKE: [pause] Well I'm one of these um – chauvinistic, um unnoticing, unobservant males who, because she's coughing a little bit, don't say, 'how are you feeling dear?' It's when she's nearly dropped dead that I realise she's got anything wrong with her.

In the same way, Richard Price had this to say in his separate interview:

CAROLINE: Do you feel that you, that you care enough about Margaret?
RICHARD: I probably do – but I don't show it. I'm sure she'd tell you that. Um – I'm just very unromantic. Terribly. I mean I don't know whether all blokes are the same, I'm sure they're not but I just – I never buy her flowers – well, very rarely. I just don't think of it. Um – it's not cause I don't want to. I just literally, come home from work, and I never think of going straight on down the shops and buying something and bringing it back. I'm just – not like that – I've never been like it. I ought to change. And you know you have a row and and you thi– oh yeah I'll change, and you never do. Well I certainly never do. So although I do care, I probably don't show it.

In this extract Richard implies that he thinks perhaps he 'should' change, only for some reason he just can't. However, as the dialogue continues, I would argue that it seems less and less likely that he does want to change:

CAROLINE: Do you think she cares about you?
RICHARD: Oh yeah, yeah. Oh I'm sure she does.
CAROLINE: Mm.
RICHARD: And she does show it I mean she'll buy me socks when she goes to shop in [town], I mean it's only little things but – it's, it's things I need – I get through a pair a week so I mean yes.
CAROLINE: Do you think men find it harder to do things like, you know, buy presents and
RICHARD: Um – I can only speak personally and I don't find it hard to buy presents I just literally don't ever think of it. Had I thou– had I though– if I thought of it then I'm sure I would er – do something about it. Um – I don't think I particularly find it difficult. I don't buy [pause] um, things like underwear and things which a lot of blokes do I mean I – wo– I wouldn't have a clue what size she was even I mean [pause] um, or even jewellery I mean I – I I'm – I wouldn't know what she particularly likes I mean it's – I know she wears simple things, but I don't um – I don't like jewellery anyway but I don't – sort of buy those sorts of things. But I well [laughing a bit] – I bought her a frying pan! [I laugh] – 'what was that for?' That went down

really well that did. I think it was her birthday, or something like that and I thought we needed a frying pan so I thought that's a good – opportunity to buy one and I bought her one [me laughing]. That was a bit silly. That didn't go down too well. Never mind.

From the above extract it seems that, far from feeling really bad about his lack of 'thought' in buying Margaret presents (he says he doesn't find it particularly difficult), Richard actually appears to be almost 'celebrating' his thoughtlessness. The fact that he can say he 'doesn't know Margaret's size', doesn't think of going to the florists and bought her such an insensitive present as a frying pan for her birthday – which he says 'didn't go down too well' – all reflects, I would argue, Richard doing the relational masculine 'I'. It is vital, I believe, to focus on the 'relational' aspect here. In all three interviews, Margaret's caring for Richard is never questioned. Richard is displaying a cavalier behaviour towards Margaret's feelings from a secure base of 'knowing' that Margaret cares enough for him. Yet Richard's behaviour clearly had dire consequences for Margaret, and in my separate interview with her she was obviously very worried about the future of their marriage.

To return to my earlier discussion of separation behaviour, one of the biggest issues between Richard and Margaret appeared to be that Richard wanted to go out without Margaret all the time – either drinking with friends, or playing sport or getting involved in his various hobbies. In Chapter 3, when talking about the use of the 'hypothetical' or general in conversation, I transcribed an extract from Margaret's dialogue in which she told me that she could not understand people wanting to go out all the time and leave their spouses at home. At that point in the dialogue she hastily told me that Richard did not do that sort of thing – and yet it was clear from other discussions with the couple that in fact he did so quite often. I believe, from talking to Margaret, that this separation behaviour of Richard's hurt her deeply. In the following extract, Richard recounts an example of such separation behaviour, and he begins by telling me that he does feel lonely sometimes and that he misses Margaret and the children if they're away:

CAROLINE: Do you ever, at all, feel lonely?

RICHARD: Feel lonely? [pause] Er yeah. Not – when we're all here. But Margaret – went down to Weymouth with her Mum – oh for a holiday a few weeks ago with the boys, and I was gonna join them, on about the third or fourth day. And I thought 'cor great! – she's going away you lucky devil, you'll be on your own for three or four days', and it was lovely for the first day. And I sat there in the evening and [pause] and by the end of the third day I was pulling my hair out. I was – er yeah I was very very lonely. I think that's the first time that – they've all gone away and left me for three or four days. And er – it was awful. I couldn't wait to get down to the caravan [in Weymouth].

CAROLINE: Yeah, right.

RICHARD: And when I got there, I wasn't exactly greeted with open arms so that was

CAROLINE: Oh dear.

RICHARD: Yeah – that was the end of that.

CAROLINE: Why was that then?

RICHARD: I can't remember w– I can't remember what that was all about? [pause] Well I was going down – that's right – they were going down there for their holiday and I could only go down for a couple of days, and I was gonna make the most of it and go birdwatching. So as soon as I arrived at 7 o'clock on the [pause] down in Weymouth – I left here at 5 [pause] long way to get down there – all I wanted to do was say good morning and – push off and go birdwatching! and that didn't go down very well! [laughing] That wan't right so.

CAROLINE: Don't you think that that was a contradiction though, the fact that you missed them?

RICHARD: [pause] Er [pause] yeah – tis I s'pose isn't it, but it was just the fact that I'd have been in th– they'd had been in Weymouth, and I was gonna be in Weymouth, and that was close enough [I laugh]. But – I was – yes, I went there for me I was – I – yeah I know what you mean. Um – I s'pose it was really. And [pause] prhaps Margaret was missing me and – [laughing a bit] when she realised I was gonna push off she was [pause] was, got a bit cross about it. So yeah I s'pose it was. But I just wanted to see them and – know they were alright and er – go birdwatching! [me laughing] Yeah, it is a contradiction. Yeah.

In the above extract, I actually challenge Richard's account and ask whether he doesn't think his behaviour was contradictory. Richard takes up the theme of contradiction and appears to agree with this. He missed them when they weren't there but when he got to Weymouth he didn't want to spend any time with them. Given his apparently contradictory behaviour any feelings of insecurity on her part would be hardly surprising. But another aspect of this account that I want to highlight here is that I believe Richard told me the story as part of his celebration of thoughtlessness regarding Margaret's needs. He did not appear to be embarrassed about constructing this version of events for me and, in fact, throughout the whole of the separate interview seemed to be quite unselfconscious about potential problems of presenting himself as selfish. (This was also the case with some of the other men I interviewed, and I will return to this point in my conclusion.) I would suggest at this juncture that – leaving the domestic labour aspect aside for now – it would have been quite difficult for Richard to continue to define the relational masculine 'I' through going out and leaving his wife at home when she wasn't there. Put another way, how could he display lack of caring when there was no safe baseline of caring from which to 'kick off'? Therefore, he had to go and find her. Furthermore, I would suggest that the construction of Margaret's insecurity served the purpose, for Richard, of potentially disempowering her. Margaret gave evidence in her interview of being a strong and determined woman who would not easily allow Richard to get his own way over day-to-day decisions concerning their lives. What better solution to keeping control of the situation for Richard, therefore, than to disempower Margaret by making her feel insecure?

Central to Richard Price's definition of himself during the interviews was a notion of aggressive machismo. He described himself to me in his separate interview as a 'typically heterosexual sort of bloke' and he was keen to emphasise his physical fitness. He also told me that on his evening sessions with his male companions, they talked about things and did things that would not 'go down too well' with Margaret if she knew. Such a construction of masculinity was clearly, from my interview data, at its heart about women's oppression. This kind of policing of the category 'male' involved making comments about partners such as 'the dragon', for example – made by Brian Thompson concerning his wife – and it seemed almost as though the more offensive such constructions could be in relation to women, the stronger the definition of masculinity. For example, in Mike Walters' transcribed extract earlier, he talked with some pride about being 'chauvinist', which meant not noticing there was anything wrong with his wife until she had 'practically dropped dead'. The implication here, I suggest, is that his 'strength' by this construction is measured by his deliberate indifference to her suffering.

By no means all of the men I interviewed made such overtly misogynist comments. About two-thirds of the men I interviewed were much more respectful, at least in the interviews. However, there was evidence in my study that the reinforcing of women's insecurity was by no means exclusively related to the men who wanted to call themselves 'chauvinists'. Take, for example, Simon Campbell. He talked about liking to 'poke fun at society' by dressing his daughters in blue instead of pink, although he also said that he thought there may well be biological differences in children causing different forms of behaviour – for example, more rough-and-tumble play in boys. Although Simon was keen to present himself to me as 'enlightened' in relation to gender politics, he was also keen to present himself as self-contained and self-sufficient and I have already discussed his lack of enthusiasm in discussing business matters with his wife, Janet. In the following extract from my separate interview with Simon, I have asked him whether he thinks he cares enough about Janet:

SIMON: [long pause] Mm – I like to think I do, but sometimes I have a – niggling doubt – that I don't – that I don't consider her, enough.

CAROLINE: In what sort of areas?

SIMON: Er [pause] considering her sort of own – considering her requirements and her needs – emotional or otherwise. Er – I might be neglectful – I might think that I'm – being neglectful. Or she might 'hint' – that I'm being neglectful [I laugh a bit].

CAROLINE: Right. Do you feel that she cares enough about you?

SIMON: Yeah I think so.

In a rather less overt way than with Richard Price's dialogue, discussed earlier, I would suggest here that although Simon seems vaguely concerned that he might not consider Janet's emotional requirements enough, what he is effectively doing is constructing a sense of masculinity through telling me that he might be neglecting her – whilst there is no question that she could be neglecting him. Furthermore, at the end of the quotation he implies that he has become aware of this neglectful behaviour through Janet pointing it out to him. Although more veiled than Mike Walters' comment that his wife would have to practically 'drop dead' before he noticed there was anything wrong, I would suggest that the same thread is running through Simon's comments. The measure of his masculinity lies in his lack of attention to his (caring) wife. The dialogue continues after a few minutes in the following way:

CAROLINE: Do you ever worry about Janet's feelings for you?
SIMON: No.
CAROLINE: Do you think she ever worries about – your feelings for her?
SIMON: Er – I get the impression she sometimes does, yes.
CAROLINE: [What, not by anything she says or?
SIMON: [But. Er – not direct – no, not by a direct comment she makes but indirectly. Um...I get an impression that she sometimes does – and needs reassurance – I think, the reassurance bit is [pause]

Although Simon suggests in the last sentence that he sometimes gets the impression she might need reassurance, as in the case of Tom Scott mentioned earlier, he does not suggest that this need for reassurance might have anything to do with his distancing behaviour and lack of consideration for her feelings. In fact, there was no serious suggestion in Simon's account that he should try to do anything to prevent his wife from feeling insecure. Rather, I would suggest that he was able to define his own self-containment and stability through her 'need for reassurance'. If he could argue that Janet needed reassurance about his feelings for her, her feelings for him could be construed as in little doubt. But more than this, if his behaviour continued to reinforce and maintain a feeling of insecurity and isolation in Janet, what better way for Simon to keep control of the agenda regarding, for example, plans for the business or, more generally, the course of their future lives?

Selfishness and masculinity

In the above analyses of dialogue with Richard Price and Simon Campbell, I have attempted to demonstrate that, within my study, evidence for men constructing women's insecurity was not confined to those men who described themselves as 'chauvinist'. In the final example of constructions of women's insecurity in this chapter, I will attempt to show that such constructions could at times be very cruel.

Before I transcribe this extract, I should point out that Gillian Henderson had given birth to the couple's third child just two weeks before I interviewed them and was feeling depressed. She is highly economically dependent on Patrick at this stage in her life. Before they had children, Patrick's earning capacity was considerably higher than Gillan's. Various themes already discussed emerge in this interview, notably, Gillian's awareness of her economic dependence; her use of a depersonalising conversation practice; woman-blame; a construction of relational closeness and Patrick sabotaging this latter construction. At this point in the interview I have just asked the couple if they have any views about why one in three marriages are currently breaking up:

PATRICK: Well I can sort of see that um [pause] getting old might frighten some people, I can see why – sort of middle-aged men go for young women [laughing a bit] – and sort of leave home and all they've got. But, you know, I can see that but [pause] it doesn't mean, I worry about it myself. Um [pause] from a woman's point – I don't know why/

GILLIAN: I think that um [pause] one in three marriages will always have broken up if it would, have been easier.

CAROLINE: Easier to do?

GILLIAN: Easier to do.

PATRICK: Mm.

[I then go on to ask the couple about the pros and cons of living together versus marriage.]

PATRICK: I was very – you know – very keen for you to keep your own maiden name and everything and [pause] you decided not to for the car insurance or something, didn't you?

GILLIAN: Yes. It got very/

PATRICK: Again it's the – you know – practicalities.

GILLIAN: very – yes. Practicalities made that um – difficult. But um/

PATRICK: And um, it was you that wanted a joint account and [pause] I suggested you have a separate account now for [pause] getting your money out and you've just done that.

[pause]

GILLIAN: It's seeing – I've seen other [pause] other women though who um [pause] you know, whose husbands have left them. [pause] I do think um – and left them with the kids and all the – you know, all the responsibilities and that sort of thing

PATRICK: Mm.

GILLIAN: and I do think it's – it's good that you have some legal redress

CAROLINE: Mm.

GILLIAN: in the– in those circumstances.

CAROLINE: Yeah.

PATRICK: Yes, but/

GILLIAN: I do feel that if, you know, if you – th– there is that commitment.

PATRICK: Mm.

[pause]

PATRICK: Oh yeah but – I – [I wouldn't have said that because the thought of us

GILLIAN: [then I think then that

PATRICK: [pause] splitting up doesn't really occur to me. It's not something I ever dwell on, whereas you – you might worry a bit more – when you think about it [slight laugh].

GILLIAN: Well yeah I cer– you know I cer– I don– I don't ever think that you're going to leave but I/

PATRICK: I've always got supreme confidence that er [pause] Gillian's not gonna go off with someone else or, get bored with me or something like that. It never occurs to me to worry about it.

CAROLINE: Mm.

PATRICK: So um [pause] you know, obviously maybe I should if [pause] if [laughing a bit] you're/

GILLIAN: No, don't worry [laughing].

PATRICK: If [you don't I'm not.

CAROLINE: [Sorry let's move – yeah [laughing]. It's only because I brought this up that you start – yeah – saying things that you/

GILLIAN: No I – I do um I, as I say I have seen other women–

PATRICK: Mm. It was interesting when we first started going out and after a couple of weeks I was saying well – do you fancy going to Holland for your holidays this summer and she said – 'Oh don't talk about that we might be split up by then!'

CAROLINE: Yeah.

PATRICK: Typ– um [pause] typifies/

CAROLINE: [to her] Well yes cause you say you're a worrier I suppose.

GILLIAN: Yeah. [Oh yes I do.

PATRICK: [Exactly yeah – it doesn't change

GILLIAN: I w– like I made him take out life insurance [laughing] cause he always assumes that he – he won't be the one that gets er [pause] knocked off his bike and killed and I think, well you know, I'll be left here with the kids you know [laughing]. 'Take out some life insurance' [laughing]

[We move on and I ask the couple what they consider to be the positive aspects of relationships.]

GILLIAN: Um [pause] I s'pose er – it is the – it is the sharing, and that – that's all there is really isn't it? [pause]

CAROLINE: Mm.

GILLIAN: Always someone who will listen and

PATRICK: Mm, that's right.

[I then ask about difficulties – in marriage in general.]

PATRICK: I s'pose fidelity's one of them isn't it. You – you're expected to remain faithful but er [pause] I don't think it's a very sort of natural thing to do. [pause] I happened to have – sort of – be faithful but um [pause] it's just um [slight laugh] no reason – there isn't a particular reason for that.
[pause]
[At this point Gillian looks as though she might burst into tears.]

CAROLINE: Do you – do you – do you see [pause] see that in that way as well?

GILLIAN: Er [pause] that it would be – that it's a problem?

CAROLINE: Yeah – that it's not necessarily a natural thing to [pause]

GILLIAN: [pause] You – you've floored me there [laughing a bit but looking upset].

PATRICK: Yeah, yeah I mean.

CAROLINE: Yeah [laughing] sorry – yeah I s'pose it is a – yeah. [pause] Often I think you kind of raise issues and then you think – you know – as I say, I do think as well that [pause] I – when I do things like th– when I go through this kind of thing myself I find I can say one thing one minute and another thing the next as well. I think that sometimes you/

PATRICK: We'll probably think up some more answers after you've gone [laughing slightly]

CAROLINE: Yeah, that's right. There's no one definitive answer for anything – no.
[pause]

GILLIAN: I think – I feel that that's probably um a – a difference, I mean i–it doesn't strike me as being a difficult thing, to be faithful.

PATRICK: It doesn't strike me as – no but er – I think that a [pause] it's something that occurs to a lot of people.

GILLIAN: It does seem to occur to other people yes [laughing – seems here as though she has rallied]. It did cross my mind when I was – when I was heavily pregnant and [laughing a bit] sex was the last thing that I wanted I did think it was a bit hard on you but

PATRICK: Mm [laughs slightly].

GILLIAN: – Yeah but...

PATRICK: (I s'pose the only thing)/

GILLIAN: You wanted the [baby as well so [laughing].

PATRICK: [That's right! No, I put that as [pause] little sacrifice.

In terms of the themes that have already been identified in this book, at the beginning of the above conversation, Gillian talks about her financial dependence on Patrick but she uses a depersonalised form to do this. Following this, he begins a construction of woman-blame and soon after this we are *all* blaming Gillian for the ensuing construction of events. I'm a prime mover here, suddenly saying to her 'well yes cause you say you're a worrier I suppose'. In this sentence, I have therefore effectively located 'the problem' of her insecure position in Gillian's disposition. It is interesting that, at this point, it was as though all three of us metaphorically 'heaved a sigh of relief' and the atmosphere lightened for a minute. It is also interesting to note that Gillian was then able to reiterate her practical/economic concerns. She then goes on to attempt a construction of relational closeness which, shortly after, Patrick Henderson seems to cruelly, and perhaps thoughtlessly, sabotage. He then constructs a version of events that seems destined to make his wife feel insecure. Given that Gillian was highly economically dependent on her husband with three young children to care for – one only two weeks old at the time of the interview – her position *was* insecure, even before Patrick started speaking. However, in the above extract, he commences by saying that he can understand older men going off with younger women (he apparently does not consider older women going off with younger men to be a possibility and this ties in with Burns and Griffin's (1996) argument that infidelity is constructed as expected or natural in men), although he doesn't worry about it himself. This comment in itself could operate to sow seeds of doubt in the listener's mind. He then proceeds to say that he doesn't think fidelity is natural, and he just 'happens' to have remained faithful. There is no particular reason why. This comment follows in the wake of Gillian trying to explain why she felt that it was important to get married and not just live together, in order that she might have legal redress if she was left with the children and it is interesting to note here that Patrick does not really give validity to her comment. On hearing his comment, Gillian looked completely stunned and about to cry. My subsequent faltering dialogue reflects my anxiety about the situation and it is also noticeable that Patrick himself seems rather uncomfortable towards the end of this extract and 'clarifies' his earlier statement to emphasise that it doesn't strike him as being difficult to be faithful – but for *other* people this might be a problem. At this point, Gillian appears to rally slightly. However, I would argue that the damage is done and that she is likely to have been left with a feeling of insecurity regarding the strength of his feelings for her. Such insecurity would obviously be disempowering and I should point out here that Gillian told me on my second visit that her depression after the birth of her third child lasted for about a year.

As I have already argued above, I suggest that creating emotional insecurity in one's partner is likely to be an effective way of keeping control over the marital agenda. I have discussed in this chapter evidence for men separating from their spouses, both physically and emotionally, and argued that such behaviour is likely to function to (1) help the husband to avoid domestic duties (2) keep control over the marital agenda by not talking – and thus avoiding the risk of verbal challenge and (3) separate self from sense of couple solidarity and hence create feelings of isolation in spouse. I further argued that this third aspect related to feelings of emotional insecurity in the women I interviewed – separation behaviour was often taken as a sign that husbands might not love them. I then examined women's insecurity in more detail and argued that there was evidence for some of the men constructing such feelings of insecurity through a form of 'celebration of thoughtlessness'. This point about celebrating thoughtlessness brings me to the second issue I want to raise here, that of husbands failing to acknowledge the validity of wives' experience.

Failing to acknowledge personal involvement – doing gender inequality

In the above extract from my interview with the Hendersons, Patrick stated that he had always had 'supreme confidence' that Gillian would not leave him. He made this comment in response to Gillian saying that she felt it was important to have some legal redress – because she had seen friends abandoned by their husbands and left to bring up the children single-handed. In his construction, Patrick omits to acknowledge that it is he that has the earning capacity and Gillian who has the child-care responsibility. Therefore, perhaps he can afford a certain amount of 'supreme confidence', whilst for Gillian, her position is more tenuous. In other words, it is through his socially privileged position that he is able to be so cavalier about Gillian's continued affection. Relatedly, his privileged position allows him to continue to construct her insecurity and disempower her. Failing to acknowledge her vulnerability therefore functions to protect and reproduce his power base. In fact, as I have already pointed out earlier in this book, most of the men I interviewed acknowledged that things might be less than equal for women in relation to the world of work. However, as I pointed out earlier, only one of the men – Bernard Hardy – acknowledged that not only might things be less than equal for women *in the marriage relationship*, but that he had to take some responsibility for men's socially constructed power and actively work to relinquish some of this power. Of the other men I interviewed, not only did none of them acknowledge that gender inequality might be anything to do with them, but eight of the men implied that things might actually be becoming rather unfair on men.

I devoted earlier chapters to a discussion of some of the ways in which I believe the men I interviewed were doing more than simply not acknowledging their involvement with women's oppression. I tried to show how I believed that most of these men were developing versions of relational identity that entrenched women's oppressed position through not just denial, but the implicit suggestion that actually their wives were quite fortunate and had an easier life than they themselves. In this connection, some of the men seemed completely incapable of seeing anybody's point of view but their own. For example, in the following short extract from my joint interview with the Freemans, I have been asking the couple for their views about the relationship between the sexes and whether or not things were becoming more equal:

NICK: I think also it's um [pause] but there again other marriages might – might be different, I mean it it's – fairly equal. I mean I think. I mean I would – I know I'm very – very sensitive, to being um, put upon, so I s'pose

> if Sally had sort of demanded more time going out and and leaving me to sort of – come home and sort of – do things with the kids – I'd probably have resented that and, felt that unfair.

Not only did Nick Freeman seem completely unselfconscious in this extract that the issue at stake in this particular discussion was women's inequality – not whether he had been 'hard done by' – but also, throughout the whole of this interview Sally had been ironing ferociously and seemed extremely stressed. She also made continual veiled references throughout the interview to her lost years of employment whilst at home with the children. I would suggest that Nick's comment functioned to try to deny the legitimacy of Sally's challenging behaviour in the interview.

A self-centred perspective – doing gender inequality

The overwhelming impression I received from my discussions with the men in my study group was of an unwillingness to see the world from their wives' perspective. This was completely the reverse with the women, who often spent a considerable time in interviews talking about their husband's perspective and apparently trying to understand their husband's problems and points of view. In this connection, I would like to outline the major aspects of what I believe were the self-centred perspectives of each man in my study:

Will Craven conveyed to me that he felt sorry for himself because he had been 'landed with' the farm that Karen's family owned.

Peter Docherty felt sorry for himself because he didn't like children and got fed up when his wife tried to make him stop watching television and play with them at the weekends. He told me that sometimes he simply refused.

Gerry Morris had been depressed for a considerable period of time. He was extremely rude to his wife in front of me in the interview and he also covertly blamed her for his depression by saying that he believed he would be well if he did not have all the responsibility of a wife and family. He did not attend the birth of their second child because he 'wanted to protect himself from being hurt' and he moved out of their bedroom while the baby was young so that he could get a good night's sleep. He told me that he had virtually nothing to do with child-care because of his depression.

Jim Wright's wife Amanda had a physical disability and Jim told me that he therefore had to help her do quite a bit in terms of housework and child-care. However, he presented this to me more in terms of a necessity linked to her handicap than as a move towards equality. Furthermore, Jim was one of the men who implied that things were in some ways becoming unfair nowadays on men.

Patrick Henderson told me in the couple's joint interview that he liked to think he could get Gillian to do things. He was 'selfish for his family'. The interview was full of evidence of Patrick constructing a sense of self at the expense of his wife – for example, he talked about the way in which he believed that men will impose and women will be put upon. In their relationship he was 'imposing for them both'. I have transcribed a long extract from the couple's joint interview above that gives a flavour of Patrick's less-than-sensitive approach to his wife's developing depression.

Neil Spencer was monosyllabic throughout the couple's joint interview. Nevertheless, he was quick to point out that Wendy did all the housework and that he himself did very little home maintenance – facts which he appeared to be almost 'celebrating'. When he had left the house – which he did rather abruptly without saying goodbye – Wendy talked at length about his separation behaviour and she was clearly unhappy about the emotional aspects of their relationship.

Brian Thompson was keen to tell me that he liked to 'make excuses' to go to the pub with his friends. He was extremely keen on sport, and talked openly, and quite proudly, about the amount of time he spent away from the home. Both spouses told me about his unfortunate habit of coming home drunk some nights – usually much later than he said he would, because I was told that he was a bad time-keeper – and urinating into the wardrobe. Cathy told me in front of Brian that she dreaded this particular behaviour.

Mike Walters was openly misogynist in his dialogue with me. He talked about the importance of the man being head of the household and his discussion – particularly in the separate interview – was disrespectful to women generally. He referred to his wife not by name but as 'the wife' and told me she would have to practically 'drop dead' before he noticed there was anything wrong with her. He called himself a chauvinist.

Malcolm Anderson was quite empathic at times in his discussion with his wife about her difficulties with her role as caregiver. However, he made no suggestion whatsoever that perhaps he could alter his behaviour to give her more support, choosing instead to attribute her problems to PMT. He furthermore pointed out that her moods could be a bit 'trying' for him at times. Malcolm was also the person who talked about finding it threatening at work when women behaved as his equal.

Simon Campbell presented himself to me as quite enlightened, choosing to dress his daughters in blue rather than pink to 'poke fun' at society. He was withdrawn in the interviews and Janet Campbell told me that he had an embarrassing tendency sometimes to walk out of the room if they had visitors, or pick up a paper if he didn't want to talk. (Once again, this kind of behaviour is echoed in the sociological literature on women's responsibility for 'social niceties'.) He was inclined to drop off to sleep most nights in the chair, both spouses told me, and he explained that he had no difficulty making a conceptual separation between family and work. However, Janet told me that she worried a great deal about Simon's business and would clearly like to have been much more involved.

Tony Matthews was quick to tell me that his wife got all the equality she wanted from him, and he felt that things might be getting a bit unfair on men.

Nick Freeman also implied that things might be becoming a bit unfair on men, and I transcribed above the extract from his dialogue where he explains that he is sensitive to being 'put upon'.

Richard Price was open in telling me that he felt 'hard done by' because he couldn't go out more on his own without his wife. The couple were in the process of visiting the doctor about his 'terrible temper' and he was keen to tell me in his separate interview that he was a 'typically heterosexual sort of bloke' who went out drinking with his friends and bought his wife a frying pan for her birthday.

Tom Scott was affable and respectful in his conversation with his wife. He did, however, tell me that he was inclined to watch rather too much television and an ongoing issue for the couple was Tom's unwillingness to socialise with Emma. Although the couple were keen to tell me that they 'mucked in together', it later transpired that Tom's major household task was the washing up and that he sometimes didn't get round to doing even this. The couple were planning to have a family in the near future and Tom explained that a role reversal would not suit him because he would not have Emma's patience.

Gordon Evans was keen to tell me that he was sure the couple had done the right thing in buying a flat for Rachael's mother rather than sending her mother to a home. This, despite the fact that Rachael had been against the idea. If he had felt this was the wrong thing to do, he pointed out, they would have had to do something about it quickly.

Bernard Hardy was the only man who made a sustained attempt to see things from his wife's perspective and, as I said earlier, take some responsibility for personal involvement in processes of gender inequality. Even he stopped short of feeling happy about a role reversal however and I have transcribed in Chapter 3 (p. 42) his rather derisory comment about 'mother and toddler groups'.

I should like to conclude this 'litany of self-centredness' with the – somewhat telling – remarks of Tim Hughes:

TIM: Didn't know women had feelings.
CAROLINE: [slight murmured laugh]
TIM: Have they?
CAROLINE: [I nod]
TIM: Oh.

CONCLUSION

In this book I have attempted to use conversation data to explore connections between identity processes, emotional experience and the dynamics of gender power relations in a wife–husband relationship. In what follows, I want to briefly summarise the main findings of my research and 'read outwards' from the lives of these married people to talk about marriages more generally.

First, my research revealed that gender inequality was 'an issue' for all the wives I interviewed and that women were actively engaged in challenging the legitimacy of perceived gender power imbalances with their husbands. In other words, these women were not content with the status quo of their relationships. This finding links with other contemporary studies suggesting that marriage has more to offer men than women (e.g. Frazier et al. 1996) and with contemporary statistics showing that women are more likely to instigate divorce than men. It also resonates with a plethora of recent articles in the popular press focusing on women's increased expectations of heterosexual relationships and the issue of whether these expectations are being met. However, although the women I interviewed were challenging inequalities in their relationships, they were – on the whole – doing this cautiously.

The caution with which women challenged gender inequalities can be significantly linked to financial dependency. A number of the women in this book had not entered marriage on an equal economic footing with their husbands. For some of the wives, marriage had clearly seemed like (and perhaps was) the best practical option for financial security in a society where gender discrimination still operates on a number of levels before marriage even enters into the picture. There is evidence that this is still likely to be the case for many young women preparing to enter adulthood in the late 1990s. Yet for all the women I interviewed, economic dependence had been either exacerbated or brought on by the birth of children and this pattern cut across class differences between the couples. All the mothers I interviewed had interrupted their full-time employment to become the main caregiver for the children – even in cases where the husbands were unemployed. It is also interesting to note that even in these cases, the wife was still effectively positioned as economically dependent because family credit was perceived by both spouses as 'his money'. In short, the women I interviewed were in a weak economic bargaining position at this point in their lives *vis-à-vis* their husbands and were aware of this. In such circumstances it is not difficult to understand why challenges to gender inequalities in relationships were rarely highly explicit or sustained.

However, as I have emphasised throughout this book, marriage is not just about economics. I have tried to show that the women in this book were not simply afraid of challenging gender inequalities in their relationships because of the practical issues at stake. The prospects of being alone or unloved were clearly lurking *emotional* terrors for the women I interviewed. It needs to be emphasised here that the need for physical and emotional intimacy, the need to be loved, respected and to belong were obviously highly important and influential considerations in most of the women's marital lives. Linked to this, I have argued throughout this book that women's views of themselves seemed to be dominated by negative feelings. In particular, feelings of insecurity, lack of confidence and guilt were common. Such negative feelings had a powerful effect of keeping women's challenges to the status quo in check. An interesting question is *why* women seemed to have such negative self-images at this time in their lives?

This brings me to the second major finding from my research. Namely, although economic dependence could obviously provide a breeding ground for such negative emotions to develop in women, this was not the whole story. Rather, negative emotions on the part of women seemed to be intimately linked to the behaviour of their husbands. In particular, there was strong evidence of husbands appearing to play on and foster wives' negative emotions in three main ways. First, through feeding back undermining images of their wife in conversational exchange. Second, through locating the blame for perceived inequalities in their wives (e.g. disposition or biology). Third, through engaging in physical and emotional distancing and separation practices with their wives. All these practices clearly had the potential to foster strong feelings of guilt, lack of confidence and insecurity amongst wives.

Of course, it needs to be emphasised here that the need for physical and emotional intimacy, the need to be loved and to belong were clearly important factors for the men I interviewed as well as the women. In fact, there is considerable evidence that marital breakdown can have dire psychological consequences for men and, in fact, is much more closely associated with depression and psychological distress in men than in women. Men frequently fall apart when divorce hits and, statistically, it is far more likely that divorce will be instigated by women than men. In such an analysis, keeping a wife insecure might start to look like a last-ditch way to avoid change and still keep her. Hence, the destruction of a wife's security could amount to the construction of a husband's.

In other words, undermining, blaming and distancing practices could be construed as central planks of a defensive or 'digging the heels in' process that husbands were engaging in as a way of trying to maintain hierarchical gender difference and thereby fend off wives' challenges and resist change. Such practices had the power to achieve this through exacerbating a wife's already vulnerable social position and, effectively, 'keep her under closer control'. I think women's challenges to gender inequalities in their relationship were being submerged in an emotional quagmire of insecurity, lack of confidence and guilt and these negative emotions were woven into the very fabric of their relationships by husbands' defensive practices. Feelings of guilt, lack of confidence and insecurity can be both debilitating and disabling and I do not think it is any coincidence that at the time of my interviews with these couples, seven of the women had in the recent past or were currently suffering from what they described as depression. Some of the other women also described feelings and experiences that sounded very similar. And it should, of course, be emphasised that the link between marriage and depression in women has been made on a number of occasions elsewhere (e.g. see Bernard 1982 and contemporary work of Ussher 1997).

Practices entered into by husbands can be explained, in psychological terms, as expressions of selfishness or self-centredness, as I argued in the previous chapter. They can also be explained, in sociological terms, as vehicles for 'doing gender inequality'.

Marriage in general

So what do the findings from this qualitative study have to say about marriages more generally? I said earlier in this book that I did not want to be guilty of making crude and inappropriate generalisations from a small group of married couples to 'married people in general'. I have argued above, nevertheless, that the circumstances of many women's lives are likely to create conditions of vulnerability similar to those experienced by the women whose lives are discussed here. Given these kinds of circumstances then, are *all* married men likely to behave in ways identified in this book? Is such behaviour inevitable? Can marriage ever be good for women? In the final sections of this book I will address some of these issues.

A likely scenario

Unfortunately, given the evidence from a variety of other sources of husbands' reluctance to change in the face of changing expectations from wives, I think it is highly *unlikely* that the destructive male practices identified in this book were a freak phenomenon of the interviews I carried out. The conditions of many women's married lives make such behaviour on the part of men all too easy. First, the institution of marriage itself frames a relationship from the outset in terms of expectations for female dependency (e.g. in the still predominant practice of women adopting the husband's name). Second, husbands in this society have at their disposal 'off the peg' woman-blaming discourses capable of making sense of a whole range of situations as 'the woman's fault'. Linked to this, there is now a considerable feminist literature attesting to the fact that selfish behaviour is much more socially acceptable in a man than a woman. Third, the notion that 'doing masculinity' should be synonymous with 'putting women down' is not exactly novel (e.g. see Edley and Wetherell 1995; Ussher 1997) and, in this analysis, a dependent wife is a potentially easy target for this kind of competitive identity work on the part of men. Finally, as Segal (1990) has commented, why should men want voluntarily to give up a power base that brings a number of privileges? So is it really very surprising that individual men may adopt underhand means to protect an unfair status quo?

But not the only possibility

It may not be surprising when husbands use their position to try to preserve the status quo. This is not to say, however, that I think such behaviour is inevitable. I do not think it is the case that all men have to, inevitably will (or are in a position to) engage in the practices identified in this book. Not only might other forms of social power potentially have confounding effects in some relationships (e.g. racism) but, also, I think it is perfectly possible for individual men to challenge sexism and tackle rather than entrench gender inequalities in their relationships – substituting equality, sharing and mutual respect for hierarchical power and privilege in their personal lives.

It has to be said, however, that caution will also need to be exercised in too easily assuming the presence of a 'new man'. Most of the men I interviewed by no means came across as straightforwardly chauvinist in interaction. They were for the most part pleasant and friendly people who expressed an interest in the issues raised. Most of them were keen at some level to present themselves as enlightened people whose relationships were characterised by values of equality and democracy. Yet, on close examination, only one man I spoke to was prepared to acknowledge that, as a man, he needed to take some personal responsibility for tackling the problem of gender inequality and recognise that this might involve some sacrifices for him in his marriage as well as his life more generally. In my view *this is the key*. The preparedness to give up material *and* emotional benefits associated with male privilege must be a fundamental requirement for becoming a real 'new man'.

In conclusion, I hope this book has demonstrated that there needs to be a lot of soul searching on the part of men concerning the relations between contemporary forms of masculinity and social power. Is it possible to transform and produce non-oppressive masculinities? What could non-hierarchical gender difference look like? What form(s) could it take? All these questions need serious attention but the debate needs to be fuelled by men's *willingness to change*. And it has to be said that if men don't demonstrate any significant willingness to change, women are likely to continue to 'vote with their feet' – a pattern already reflected in contemporary divorce statistics. In other words, if men don't participate willingly in a renegotiation of gender power relations, material and emotional privileges are nevertheless likely to be eroded for men through the 'fall-out' of marital breakdown and divorce.

Two final points on the future of heterosexual relations need to be made before closing this book.

First, there is the issue of the marriage contract. Despite the fact that entering into marriage can sometimes seem like a sensible financial option for women (e.g. because of factors such as pension rights and maintenance payments in the event of relationship breakdown) I think that such an institution/legal contract can, in the long run, only act as a barrier to women's equality. This is because the institution frames the relationship at the outset in terms of women's dependency and makes it hard for a woman to retain an independent sense of identity in the eyes of family, friends and society at large. I think it is a necessary but not sufficient condition of a long-term swing towards gender equality that heterosexual women resist the contract and allow themselves some space to define gender and personal identity in more liberating and non-traditional ways. If the marriage statistics are anything to go by, this swing is already under way. However, the second point relates to the problem of post-feminism.

Post-feminism, I think, presents a particular threat to tackling gender inequalities in an area that is already fraught with the sensitivities and complications discussed throughout this book. As teaching has brought home to me, we are moving into an age where young women are not comfortable using the language of the women's liberation movement or talking too openly about gender in connection with social power and oppression – *particularly* in the context of heterosexual relationships. Books such as Gray's *Men are from Mars, Women are from Venus* (1997) and Tannen's *You Just Don't Understand Me* (1990) have been immensely popular and the language of 'communication breakdown' and 'misunderstanding' has captured the moment in the so called post-feminist 1990s. The 'two cultures theory' of gender difference (the notion that women and men misunderstand each other because they have effectively been socialised in completely different sub-cultures) has an optimistic and non-confrontational feel to it. If it's a misunderstanding, problems are relatively easily resolved. There is no dangerous sub-text. On the contrary, the 'fall-out' from such misunderstanding is a kind of innocent confusion – often demonstrated in TV situation comedies such as *Men Behaving Badly*. Perhaps the language of misunderstanding and sub-cultural difference can allow the possibility for a wife to tackle gender power relations in a non-threatening way and, equally, for a husband to back down without loss of face – if he wants to. However, the 'innocent confusion' model of interpersonal communication in marriage bears little resemblance to the worlds of the married couples discussed in this book. Furthermore, the ascendance of such a theory in the popular mind makes it even more likely that a wife experiencing deep-seated gender inequalities within a marriage will find it impossible to articulate such problems. In the popular 'cereal packet' notion of marriage we have moved into an age where the relationship is *supposed to be* enshrined in values of democracy and equality. In such circumstances, awareness that personal reality does not seem to match societal ideals could become a kind of 'guilty secret' as I think it was for many of the women I interviewed. Post-feminism is likely to compound a 'guilty secret' where personal experiences do not match up to public expectations. When it comes to marriage and heterosexual relationships, we certainly cannot afford to become post-feminist yet.

NOTES

1 A FEMINIST PSYCHOLOGICAL APPROACH TO MARRIAGE RESEARCH

1 See Office for National Statistics *Social Trends* 1998 edition, London: Verso for a detailed breakdown of marriage and divorce statistics.

2 The 1996 Family Law Act introduced 'no fault divorce' after one year rather than two and removed the possibility of proving breakdown through fault. An initial proposed compulsory 'cooling off period' of one year was overturned and now stands at eighteen months. For more information on the Bill, see Family Policy Studies Centre, Family Briefing Paper 1, March 1996.

2 A FEMINIST BIOGRAPHY OF MARRIED COUPLES

1 I have used pseudonyms throughout and changed certain details in order to protect people's identities.

2 Half of my participants were obtained through making contact with a play-group in an inner-city area and asking all the parents who were there on that day (all women) if they would be prepared to participate. All but one (who told me her husband would not agree) spoke to their husbands and then agreed to participate as a couple. The other half of my participants was obtained through sending out a letter through a local GP. I did not know who the GP sent letters to and, if the couple were interested in participating, the onus was on them to contact me.

4 HUSBANDS AND THE STRUGGLE TO DEFEND RELATIONAL INEQUALITY

1 Bell and Newby's theoretical paper, written two decades ago, has particular relevance here. They posited two opposing processes relevant to a marital relationship, the first termed 'differentiation' and the second 'identification'. By 'differentiation', Bell and Newby were referring to a husband's attempts to draw a hierarchical gender boundary between self and spouse within the marriage. By 'identification', the authors were referring to an apparently opposing process involving the breaking down of this boundary in order to foster closeness and solidarity between the couple. By this account a married man, in order to protect his gendered power base, will need to *tension manage* opposing processes of differentiation and identification in order to effectively 'do social power'.

REFERENCES

Anderson, B.S. and Zinsser, J.P. (1988) *A History of their Own: Women in Europe from Prehistory to the Present*, Vol. 11, London: Penguin.

Baber, K.M. and Allen, K.R. (1992) *Women and Families: Feminist Reconstructions*, London: The Guilford Press.

Backett, K.C. (1982) *Mothers and Fathers. A Study of the Development and Negotiation of Parental Behaviour*, London: Macmillan.

Barrett, M. And McIntosh, M. (1982) *The Anti-Social Family*, London: Verso.

Beck, U. (1992) *The Risk Society*, London: Sage.

Beechey, V. (1987) *Unequal Work*, London: Verso.

Bell, C. And Newby, H. (1976) 'Husbands and Wives: the Dynamics of the Deferential Dialectic', in D. Barker And H. Allen (eds) *Dependence and Exploitation in Marriage*, London: Longman.

Berger, P.L. and Kellner, H. (1964) 'Marriage and the Construction of Reality', in M. Anderson (ed.) *Sociology of the Family*, Harmondsworth: Penguin, 1982.

Berger, P.L. and Luckmann, T. (1966) *The Social Construction of Reality*, Harmondsworth: Penguin.

Berk, S. Fenstermaker (1985) *The Gender Factory: The Apportionment of Work in American Households*, New York: Plenum.

Bernard, J. (1982) *The Future of Marriage*, New York: Yale University Press, second edition.

Bhavnani, K.K. and Pheonix, A. (1994) *Shifting Identities Shifting Racisms*, London: Sage.

Billig, M. (1991) *Ideology and Opinions*, London: Sage.

Billinghurst, B. (1996) 'Theorising Women's Self-blame', *Feminism and Psychology*, 6 (4) pp. 569–573.

Brittan, A. (1989) *Masculinity and Power*, Oxford: Blackwell.

Bruess, C.J.S. and Pearson, J.C. (1996) 'Gendered Patterns in Family Communication', in J.T. Wood (ed.) *Gendered Relationships*, California: Mayfield Publishing.

Burman, E. (ed.) (1990) *Feminists and Psychological Practice*, London: Sage.

Burns, A. and Griffin, C. (1996) 'Constructing Accounts of Infidelity in Heterosexual Relationships', Paper presented at the Annual Conference of the British Psychological Society, University of Strathclyde, September.

Burr, V. (1995) *An Introduction to Social Constructionism*, London: Routledge.

Clark, D. (ed.) (1991) *Marriage, Domestic Life and Social Change: Writings for Jacqueline Burgoyne (1944–88)*, London: Routledge.

Coward, R. (1993) *Our Treacherous Hearts*, London: Faber and Faber.

Coyle, A. (1984) *Redundant Women*, London: The Women's Press.

Cunningham-Burley, S. (1984) 'We Don't Talk About It…! Issues of Gender and Method in the Portrayal of Grandfatherhood', *Sociology* 18 (3) pp. 325–338.

DeFransisco, V.L. (1991) 'The Sounds of Silence: How Men Silence Women in Marital Relations', *Discourse and Society* 2 (4) pp. 413–424.

Delphy, C., and Leonard, D. (1992) *Familiar Exploitation: A New Analysis of Marriage in Contemporary Western Societies*, Cambridge: Polity Press.

DeVault, M.L. (1991) *Feeding the Family: The Social Organisation of Caring as Gendered Work*, Chicago: University of Chicago Press.

Duelli-Klein, R. (1983) 'How We Do What We Want To Do: Thoughts About Feminist Methodology', in G. Bowles and R. Duelli-Klein (eds) *Theories of Women's Studies*, London: Routledge.

Duncombe, J. and Marsden, D. (1993) 'Love and Intimacy: The Gender Division of Emotion and Emotion Work', *Sociology*, 27 (2) pp. 221–242.

—— (1995) 'Workaholics and Whingeing Women: The Last Frontiers of Gender Inequality', *The Sociological Review*, 43 (1) pp. 150–169.

—— (1996) 'Can We Research the Private Sphere? Methodological and Ethical Problems in the Study of the Role of Intimate Emotion in Personal Relationships', in L. Morris and E.S. Lyon (eds), *Gender Relations in Public and Private*, Basingstoke: Macmillan.

Edley, N. and Wetherell, M. (1995) *Men in Perspective: Practice, Power and Identity*, Hemel Hempstead: Prentice Hall/Harvester Wheatsheaf.

Edwards, D. and Potter, J. (1992) *Discursive Psychology*, London: Sage.

Finch, J. (1983) *Married to the Job*, London: Allen and Unwin.

Frazier, P., Arikian, N., Benson, S., Losoff, A. and Maurer, S. (1996) 'Desire for Marriage and Life Satisfaction among Unmarried Heterosexual Adults', *Journal of Social and Personal Relationships*, 13 (2) pp. 225–240.

Friedan, B. (1965) *The Feminine Mystique*, Harmondsworth: Penguin.

Frosh, S. (1989) *Psychoanalysis and Psychology: Minding the Gap*, Basingstoke: Macmillan.

Gavron, H. (1966) *The Captive Wife: Conflicts of Housebound Mothers*, London: Routledge and Kegan Paul.

Giddens, A. (1992) *The Transformation of Intimacy*, Cambridge: Polity.

Giorgi, A. (1970) *Psychology as a Human Science: A Phenomenologically Based Approach*, New York: Harper Row.

Goffman, E. (1982) *The Presentation of Self in Everyday Life*, Harmondsworth: Penguin.

Gottman, J.M. and Levenson, R.W. (1986) 'The Social Psychophysiology of Marriage', in P. Noller and M. Fitzpatrick (eds) *Perspectives on Marital Interaction*, College Hill Press.

Gray, J. (1997) *Men are from Mars, Women are from Venus*, London: HarperCollins.

Griffin, C. (1989) 'I'm not a Women's Libber but… Feminism, Consciousness and Identity', in S. Skevington and D. Baker (eds) *The Social Identity of Women*, London: Sage.

—— (1985) *Typical Girls? Young Women from School to the Job Market*, London: Routledge and Kegan Paul.

Hale, Rt. Hon. Mrs Justice (1997) *Public Lives and Public Duties*, The 8th ESRC Annual Lecture.

Hamilton, C. (1909) *Marriage as a Trade*, London.

Henriques, J., Hollway, W., Urwin, C., Venn, C., and Walkerdine, V. (1984) *Changing the Subject*, London: Methuen.

Henwood, K, and Pidgeon, N. (1995) 'Remaking the Link: Qualitative Research and Feminist Standpoint Theory', *Feminism and Psychology*, 5 (1) 7–30.

Hogg, M. and Abrams, D. (1988) *Social Identifications*, London: Routledge.

Hollway, W. (1989) *Subjectivity and Method in Psychology*, London: Sage.

Hunt, P (1980) *Gender and Class Consciousness*, London: Macmillan.

Kitzinger, C. (1987) *The Social Construction of Lesbianism*, London: Sage.

Kitzinger, C. and Powell, D. (1995) 'Engendering Infidelity: Essentialist and Social Constructionist Readings of a Story Completion Task', *Feminism and Psychology* 5 (3) pp. 345–372.

Lewis, C. and O'Brien, M. (eds) (1987) *Reassessing Fatherhood: New Observations on Fathers and the Modern Family*, London: Sage.

Mansfield, P. and Collard, J. (1988) *The Beginning of the Rest of Your Life? A Portrait of Newly-Wed Marriage*, Basingstoke: Macmillan.

Mason, J. (1987) 'A Bed of Roses? Women, Marriage and Inequality in Later Life', in P. Allat, T. Keil, A. Bryman, and B. Bytheway (eds), *Women and the Life Cycle*, Basingstoke: Macmillan.

—— (1996) 'Gender, Care and Sensibility in Family and Kin Relationships', in J. Holland and L. Adkins (eds), *Sensibility and the Gendered Body*, London: Macmillan.

McKee, L. and O'Brien, M. (1983) 'Interviewing Men: Taking Gender Seriously', in E. Gamarnikow, D. Morgan, J. Purvis and D. Taylorson (eds), *The Public and the Private*, London: Heinemann.

Mead, G.H. (1934) *Mind, Self and Society*, Chicago: University of Chicago Press.

Nicolson, P. (1996) *Gender, Power and Organisation: A Psychological Perspective*, London: Routledge.

Oakley, A. (1974) *Housewife*, Harmondsworth: Penguin.

Pahl, J. (1989) *Money and Marriage*, Basingstoke: Macmillan.

Philips, A. and Taylor, B. (1980) 'Sex and Skill: Notes Towards a Feminist Economics', *Feminist Review*, 6.

Phoenix, A., Woollett, A, and Lloyd, E. (1991) *Motherhood: Meanings, Practices and Ideologies*, London: Sage.

Potter, J. and Wetherell, M. (1987) *Discourse and Social Psychology: Beyond Attitudes and Behaviour*, London: Sage.

Press, J.E. and Townsley, E. (1998) 'Wives' and Husbands' Housework Reporting: Gender, Class and Social Desirability', *Gender and Society*, 12 (2) pp. 188–218.

Rodger, J.J. (1996) *Family Life and Social Control: A Sociological Perspective*, Basingstoke: Macmillan.

Rowbotham, S. (1973) *Women's Consciousness, Men's World*, Harmondsworth: Penguin.

Schneider, C. (1990) 'The Struggle Towards a Feminist Practice in Family Therapy: Practices', in R.J. Perelberg and A.C. Miller (eds), *Gender and Power in Families*, London: Routledge.

Segal, L. (1990) *Slow Motion: Changing Masculinities, Changing Men*, London: Virago.

Seligman, M.E.P. (1974) 'Depression and Learned Helplessness', in R.J. Friedman and M.M. Katz (eds), *The Psychology of Depression: Contemporary Theory and Research*, Washington: V.H. Winston.

Smith, D. (1990) *The Conceptual Practices of Power: A Feminist Sociology of Knowledge*, Toronto: University of Toronto Press.

Squire, C. (1989) *Significant Differences*, London: Routledge.

Tannen, D. (1990) *You Just Don't Understand: Women and Men in Conversation*, New York: William Morrow.

Urry, A. (1990) 'The Struggle Towards a Feminist Practice in Family Therapy: Premises', in R.J. Perelberg and A.C. Miller (eds) *Gender and Power in Families*, London: Routledge.

Ussher, J. (1991) *Women's Madness: Misogyny or Mental Illness?*, Brighton: Harvester Wheatsheaf.

—— (1997) *Fantasies of Femininity*, London: Penguin.

Van Every, J. (1995) *Heterosexual Women Changing the Family: Refusing to be a Wife*, London: Taylor and Francis.

Walkerdine, V., Lucy, H. and Melody, J. (1997) *Transitions to Womanhood*, London: Macmillan.

Watson, J.B. (1924) *Behaviourism*, New York: Norton.

Weedon, C. (1987) *Feminist Practice and Poststructuralist Theory*, Oxford: Blackwell.

West, C. and Zimmerman, D. (1991) 'Doing Gender', in J. Lorber and S.A. Farrell (eds), *The Social Construction of Gender*, Newbury Park: Sage.

Wetherell, M. and Potter, J. (1991) *Mapping the Language of Racism*, Hemel Hempstead: Harvester Wheatsheaf.

Wilkinson, S. (ed.) (1986) *Feminist Social Psychology*, London: Sage.

Wilkinson, S. and Kitzinger, C. (eds) (1995) *Feminism and Discourse*, London: Sage.

Williams, J.A. (1984) 'Gender and Intergroup Behaviour: Towards an Integration', *British Journal of Psychology*, 23, pp. 311–316.

Witz, A. (1993) 'Women at Work', in D. Richardson and V. Robinson (eds) *Introducing Women's Studies*, London: Macmillan.

Wood, J.T. (ed.) (1996) *Gendered Relationships*, London: Mayfield Publishing.

INDEX OF COUPLES

INDEX OF NAMES AND SUBJECTS